HARDPRESS.NET
HOME OF HARD-TO-FIND BOOKS

Temptation and Atonement, and Other Tales
by Catherine Grace F. Gore

47. 9/79.

TEMPTATION

AND

ATONEMENT,

AND OTHER TALES.

BY

MRS. GORE,

AUTHOR OF "MEN OF CAPITAL," "THE BANKER'S WIFE,"
ETC., ETC.

IN THREE VOLUMES.

VOL. II.

LONDON:

HENRY COLBURN, PUBLISHER,

GREAT MARLBOROUGH STREET.

1847.

F. Shoberl, Jun., Printer to H.R.H. Prince Albert, Rupert Street.

CONTENTS

OF

THE SECOND VOLUME.

	PAGE
Judge Not, that ye be not Judged	1
A Passage in the Civil Wars	60
A Vision of a Royal Ball	106
An Account of a Creditor	159
The Hot Water Cure	220
May Fair at Bruges	274
Hush!	303

JUDGE NOT, THAT YE BE NOT JUDGED.

Among our minor garrisons of the Mediterranean, one, which we shall describe under the name of Z——, enjoyed, five-and-twenty years ago, a far from enviable reputation. The climate was pronounced to be unhealthy, the colony odious—one of those united populations of Greek, Italian, English, and nondescript, which poverty, dirt, bigotry, and a harbour, amalgamate into everything that is unrecommendable.

Though the island was known to be diversified by lovely scenery, and the bay to afford attraction to yachting dandies, a regiment under orders for Z—— was sure to exhaust itself in grumbling previous to embarkation;

B

and if it happened to contain a stray honourable or baronet,—Sir George or Sir Thomas, —or the Honourable Lionel So-and-so, was equally sure to be gazetted into some Brightonized regiment of hussars, "vice Lieutenant John Brown, or Ensign Thomas Smith, who exchanges."

In process of time, however, the Thomas Smiths and John Browns, so exchanging, began to describe the colony, in their letters homeward-bound, in such glowing terms, that it became clear a golden age had dawned for the garrison. The climate had become salubrious, the roads excellent, the society pleasant—with cricket-matches and races, private theatricals and balls in due season, to enliven the tedium of exile. It was observed, moreover, that the English yachts dropping anchor in the lovely little bay, appeared to find far more difficulty in getting under weigh again, than at Athens or Valetta.

These improvements were of course ascribable to the influence of a guardian genius, in the shape of a governor. Sir George Harcourt was a man of good fortune, good sense, and good temper—who, thus secured against the two sunken rocks of governors and government-houses in military colonies, viz., stinginess, in order to lay by fortunes for a young family, or prodigality, in order to conciliate the good word of fashionable cruizers, —devoted himself to promote the welfare of Z——.

Like all reformers, his early efforts were hailed with considerable dissatisfaction on the part of a lazy colonel of engineers, who had been undergoing a slow process of desiccation for the preceding ten years, under the influence of the tropical sun and a tertian ague; and reports were privately despatched home, of a terrible mortality among the troops under the command of Lieutenant-general Sir George Harcourt, K.C.B., produced in the process of draining a fetid marsh adjoining the town, and improving the harbour.

At the close of five years, however, the lazy colonel became superannuated, and Sir George Harcourt had thenceforward the comfort of a more active coadjutor. The town prospered—its commerce was nearly doubled —and the white and sun-baked walls of Z——, with the striped awnings of its balconies, assumed a more cheerful aspect as the population became healthy and active.

All this time, the governor had been leading a bachelor-life, which perhaps tended not a little to its activity and usefulness. He had originally accepted the appointment as an excuse for escaping from England and the grief of losing a beloved wife; and the two little daughters bequeathed by her to his affection had been ever since at school, under the authority of his maiden sister.

More than once, indeed, he had visited his native country in the interim, to enjoy a sight of his two promising girls. But he loved them too well to desire that they should share his exile till their education was completed, and Z—— brought to the degree of amelioration indispensable to their welfare.

The Harcourt family, however, was unanimous in advising, as Emma and Sophia approached their sixteenth and seventeenth years, that he should resign his appointment and settle with them in England. But the General was unpersuadable. During the ten years he had resided at Z———, the colony had become, as it were, a third child to him! He loved it with all the force of the favours he had conferred upon the place; and as the two girls had luckily imbibed from their father's letters considerable interest in his seat of government, so far from regarding a sojourn there as banishment, they were enchanted at the thoughts of accompanying Sir George to the Mediterranean, at the close of a London season in which he had visited England in order to witness Sophia's presentation at court.

Even Aunt Martha, who had made sundry difficulties about undertaking so unspinster-like a change as to preside over the government-house of a military colony, at length consented to accompany the dear girls, rather than leave them exposed to the perils and dangers of a trying situation.

Thanks to the facilitation of steam, the voyage was happily accomplished; and for many weeks succeeding their arrival, the half Oriental beauties of that lovely island transported the inexperienced English girls into the regions of romance. They were quiet ready to subscribe to the opinion of the Ensign Smiths and Lieutenant Browns, that Z—— was a paradise upon earth!

Aunt Martha, unluckily, was far from sharing their opinion. The tranquillity of her villa at Campden Hill had not prepared her for the drummings and fifings, the parades, and morning and evening guns, of military government, and she had not been a month in the garrison, before the sight of a red coat was as much a source of ire and irritation to her, as to a turkey-cock.

It was in vain that she discharged against her excellent brother her quiver of maidenly pruderies. More amused than angry, he would not hear of depriving himself of the society of his darling girls, and immuring them in Mahommedan seclusion, because he was occasionally surrounded with handsome aides-de-camp, and gallant brigade-majors.

"I don't ask you to appear at table on public days," said he, in reply to Aunt Martha's lamentations over the destiny of her nieces. "I don't want you or the girls to figure at reviews. But I have lived too long debarred from their company, to coincide in your wish that they should reside all the year round at Santa Chiara, instead of the government-house. No, no!—In the hot season, we will all remove to the villa together, and, in winter-time, remain together at Z——. The girls will enjoy themselves tolerably, I make no doubt. Last Christmas, the officers of the ——th got up the 'School for Scandal' in first-rate style; and though the Greek ladies might not pass muster at Almacks, I promise you, that the ball of the French consul, last winter, was one of the prettiest entertainments I ever saw in my life!"

"But all these officers, my dear brother! —Perpetually officers—whichever way one turns, *nothing* but officers!"——

"What then?——Am I not an officer my-self?——and a more gentlemanly set of young men than those under my command, I defy you to produce.——Has any one of them done any thing to offend you, sister?"

Aunt Martha, whose ungraciousness had prevented every officer of the garrison from approaching her within two hundred paces, resented the supposition with becoming dignity.

"I only mean to say," she resumed, "that there can be no call upon you to entertain at your table, as you do, all the subalterns of Z——; or at all events, none to compel your daughters and myself to appear at table in these heterogeneous parties."

"My dear sister Martha," cried Sir George, more peremptorily than he was in the habit of addressing her, "I make it a rule to behave towards the young men in this garrison, who are recommended to me either by private introduction or their personal merit, as I should wish a son of my own to be treated, under the same circumstances. With respect to the girls, I think too highly of their taste and principles to suppose their affections at the mercy of the first good-looking fellow in epaulettes, who tries to make himself acceptable ; and flatter myself I command too much respect here, to admit of any officer of the garrison pressing upon them attentions that are *un*acceptable.——They are a soldier's daughters, and, consequently, not above becoming soldiers' wives ; and though you fancy that Sophy has a sneaking kindness for her cousin Gerard Harcourt, now that she is out of the way of seeing his fine park, and reading his fine speeches, it would not surprise me at all if she were to——"

" Now, my dear, *dear* George !——For goodness' sake do not threaten me again with that horrible aide-de-camp of yours,——that dreadful Captain Orde," cried the prim maiden lady.

" Pho, pho, pho ! I only reserve Bob Orde to frighten you with, when you put on your stiffest buckram !"——cried her brother. " How do you know that I was not going to talk about Lord Algernon Spray, or some other of

the milk-and-water yachting sprigs of nobility, of whom you are so fond ?"

Aunt Martha soon saw that her case was
hopeless. The habits of the frank-hearted
soldier were unreformable. To his social
round table, the young men of the garrison
were successively invited; and the consequence was that the two accomplished girls
they were permitted to approach so nearly,
had no difficulty in discerning how few among
them possessed the refinement of manners and
cultivation of mind that might have rendered
their society dangerous. Many a showy
captain, attractive enough when viewed from
a distance, lost all charm in crossing the
magic threshold of the drawing-room of the
government-house.

On the other hand, the governor's two
handsome and pleasing daughters became of
course the divinities of the island. With
half the attractions they exhibited, the popularity of Sir George's family was pre-assured.
But they possessed merit inherent as well as
inherited; and it came to pass that the letters

to England of the Lieutenant Browns and the
Ensign Smiths, as well as the revelations of
dandy yachters and fashionable tourists described in such glowing colours the cheerful-
ness of a winter at Z——, and the beauties
of the villa of Santa Chiara, that *now*, instead
of the Honourable Lionels selling out of a
regiment ordered to that orange-growing
colony, commissions were at a considerable
premium !——

By degrees, even Aunt Martha reconciled
herself to " the spirit-stirring drum and ear-
piercing fife ;" and had founded a variety of
charitable institutions in the garrison, tending to prove that with all her antipathy to
the red-coats, their wives and families were
as acceptable to her Good-Samaritanism, as
those of Campden Hill. She was perhaps
the more encouraged to humanity, because
neither her own apprehensions nor the predictions of the General were verified. So far
from showing the smallest favour to her
father's jolly aide-de-camp, Sophia was as
faithful as ever to the Debates ; and the

framed and glazed portrait of Harcourt Hall which hung in her dressing-room at Santa Chiara; while as to Emma, she seemed to take no more heed of the gallant ——th and ——th than if they had been a confraternity of Capuchins !——

It happened that, while spending their second summer at Santa Chiara (a charming marine villa at the back of the island, to which only a few of the more favoured officers were invited by Sir George), an accident of a serious nature befel the government steam-packet as it entered the harbour of Z——; and the next time Captain Orde (the jolly aide-de-camp so much an object of abhorrence to Aunt Martha) visited the villa, he was vehement in praise of the presence of mind and gallantry displayed on the occasion by a certain Captain Fairfax, who was come out to join the ——th, and had, on the sad occasion, lost all his baggage, and preserved several lives.

"*Who* is he—*what* is he?" was the universal exclamation; to which Bob Orde, who was a privileged favourite with Sir George, was pleased to answer that he was " a deuced good-looking fellow,——but shy and sentimental as a girl."——

" Which means, probably, that he is a young man of modest and amiable manners !" retorted Aunt Martha.

" All that, and a trifle more, my dear madam !"——cried the jolly aide-de-camp. " It means that though Fairfax must have been reduced to grievous *shifts* by his want of *shirts,* and other deficiencies arising from the loss of his baggage, not one of us could get him to accept the smallest civility at our wardrobes ! ——Though reduced to linen as coarse as a mainsail, he persisted in holding us at bay."

" Did he bring letters to me ?"——inquired Sir George, not noticing the glum looks of his sister.

" To no one !"——replied the aide-de-camp. " He got into the regiment I fancy through the Horse-guards. He seems a gentlemanly man and smart officer, which, at present, is all we know of him."

Before a month elapsed, however, they knew *much* more. The first time Sir George Harcourt visited——, he was so captivated by all he heard of the courage and energy exhibited, at the moment of the wreck by the young soldier, as to invite him to accompany him back to Santa Chiara.

" Did you ever hear any thing so preposterous!" cried one of the Lieutenant Browns, that day at mess, to one of the Ensign Smiths; " the General actually invited Fairfax at parade this morning to go back with him for a few days to Santa Chiara!"

" I suppose he brought letters to the Harcourts ?"——

" Not he!——If he *did*, all his papers went to the bottom. But he told me himself, yesterday, he had no introduction to any officer in the garrison."

" Well, they will all be glad enough to know him if the governor takes him by the hand. He was a hero before he landed ! and by the time he comes from the Santa Chiara, there will be no living in the same barracks with him!"—cried Ensign Smith, who cherished an unhappy passion for the governor's youngest daughter.

"But who talked about his coming back! —He is not gone yet!—he is not even going. —He excused himself to Sir George Harcourt with the air of a grandee of Spain!"

"Fairfax *declined* an invitation to Santa Chiara?"

"Why not?—He has never seen, and perhaps never heard of, the *real* attractions of the place. So he pleaded want of clothes, —or want of spirits,—or want of inclination, —or want of something or other—"

"And Sir George, I suppose, took it all in his usual good part! Where the old fellow takes a fancy, his indulgence is quite absurd!—I should like to see you or I refuse an invitation to his country-house!"

"*I* should be quite content to hear it *given!*"—replied the other, good humouredly. "However, I dined at the government-house four times last winter, which is more than I had a right to expect; and as to Santa

Chiara, all the music and sketching and reading aloud, which they say goes on there from morning till night, would bore *me* to death. My cigar and game at billiards here at Z—— suit me a cursed deal better!"

That Sir George Harcourt took in good part the refusal of the new lieutenant to join his family circle was more than true. He was, in fact, most agreeably impressed by Fairfax's grave and graceful deportment, and spoke of him on his return to the villa in terms so favourable, that even aunt Martha began to feel interested in the hero of the wreck.

"If my brother had not described him as so young and good-looking," said she, "I should have felt inclined to propose our devoting our needles to replace a portion of the wardrobe lost by his humane exertions in behalf of others. But so unusually handsome as this Captain Fairfax is said to be, my dears, our motives might possibly be misinterpreted."

"More likely," observed Sophia, "our

offering might be as ungraciously rejected as that of poor Captain Orde!—All we hear of this new comer is his aptitude in saying ' no.' "—

" Sophy is always thinking of the ' ayes' and ' noes!' "—was the sly rejoinder of her sister Emma.

" On the contrary, I was thinking only that respect for my father ought to have insured acceptance of his invitation," replied Miss Harcourt, haughtily; and already she appeared to have conceived a prejudice against the new comer.

They had soon an opportunity of judging for themselves of his attractions.

During the frequent absences of Sir George from Santa Chiara for the execution of his official duties, the two girls were in the habit of enjoying very early or very late rides, either before sunrise or after sunset, escorted by an old English groom, who had been twenty years in the service of Sir George; and about a week after the period in question they were tempted by the beauty and freshness of a fine morning after a long continuance of rain to pursue their ride as far as some mineral springs at the distance of half-a-dozen miles from the villa, situated in the gorge of the lovely valley of Bocchetta, which had more than once afforded subjects for their pencil.

" The myrtles at Bocchetta will look so green and beautiful after the rain !" said Emma, while persuading her sister to prolong their ramble; and having reached the cliffs, richly thicketed with evergreens, which afforded so pleasant a relief to the dingy olive plantations surrounding Santa Chiara, they prepared to dismount, as they had often done before, at a goatherd's cottage adjoining the springs, to obtain water for their horses and refreshment for themselves.

To their great embarrassment, the little house was already occupied. A stranger was stretched asleep on its wooden bench, whom a wallet placed beside him on the ground, and the geological specimens scattered upon the rude table on which they had intended to breakfast, pointed out as a tourist; and before the girls could accomplish their purpose of escaping without disturbing the sleeper, the shout of joy with which the governor's daughters were recognized by the goatherd's wife, who was plying her spindle in the corner, caused the stranger to start to his feet.

Mutual apologies were exchanged; for as the girls stood with their habits gathered up for a hasty retreat, and the young stranger, colouring to the temples, appeared transfixed by sudden idiotism, they mutually recognized each other as English by this instinctive shyness. Foreigners of almost any other nation would have been prompted by an encounter in that secluded spot, to instant association. Scarcely, however, had the Miss Harcourts crossed the threshold of the hovel for departure, when the recollection that it was the province of their father's daughters to fulfil the duties of hospitality towards their country people visiting the island, induced them to return and inquire whether the stranger were aware that better accommodation was to be procured at a village, a mile or two nearer the coast, than among the scattered hovels of Bocchetta?——

" I slept last night at Pietrone," was his embarrassed reply. " This excursion having simply a scientific object, I am not difficult as to my accommodations. These hospitable people have afforded me the best shelter and refreshments at their disposal, and I am content."

The constrained manners of the stranger rendered it difficult for Miss Harcourt to pursue towards him her hospitable intentions. From the deferential manner in which he stood uncovered to answer her, she entertained little doubt that they were recognized ; and was again about to withdraw from the conference, when Emma, who had suspicious of her own concerning the identity of the stranger, frankly interposed.

" You cannot have been long on the island, or you would have visited Bocchetta before," said she, " for every one who comes to Z—— hastens hither. Bocchetta is always the first object of travellers. I suspect, therefore, that we have the pleasure of addressing Captain Fairfax ?"

An air of awkward surprise accompanied the affirmative bow of the stranger; and when Miss Harcourt, some time afterwards, reproved her sister for the abruptness of her apostrophe, she did not fail to add that he looked far more amazed than gratified by the recognition.

" I trust the difficulties which prevented our having the pleasure of seeing you last week at Santa Chiara are so far removed," added Emma Harcourt, " that you will not be thus near us without favouring my father with a visit ?—He has been surveying the new Cape road. But we expect him home this evening."

" It would mortify him much to know that you had visited Bocchetta without extending your tour to his villa," added Miss Harcourt, more formally; and though the young Englishman persisted that his travelling knapsack contained only a change of

linen, and that to present himself at the
governor's was impossible, by the time the
Miss Harcourts had done the honours of the
springs, received his instructions on the stra-
tification of Bocchetta, shared with him the
bread and salt of the goatherd's cottage, and
wandered among the myrtle thickets, while
old Robert eased the girths of their ponies
in the shade, he had become a convert to
their opinion that, with the aid of the habili-
ments always left by Captain Orde at the
villa, he might permit himself to accept their
offered hospitality.

"If you would not mind accompanying us
on foot as far as Pietrone," was Emma Harcourt's amendment on the motion, "you
might mount Robert's horse back to Santa
Chiara, and he could borrow the miller's
mule."

Even this friendly proposal, though at first
declined, was eventually accepted ; and the
mild, gentlemanly manners of Arthur Fairfax soon placed them so thoroughly at ease,
that the pleasure they had at first experienced

from meeting a countryman in the wilderness, and hearing their native language spoken among the myrtle groves of Bocchetta, gave way to the higher satisfaction of having made an agreeable acquaintance.

It was not till they discerned, at a turning of the road, the lofty cypresses overtopping the white walls of Santa Chiara, it occurred at the same moment to Emma and Sophia, that their unceremonious invitation, and the appearance in their company of a strange young man in a fustian shooting-jacket, might produce a frown on the demure face of Aunt Martha!—

To their great relief, the first person who accosted them on entering the gateway was the jocular aide-de-camp! The General, he informed them, had stolen a march upon them, and was already arrived. Leaving, therefore, to Captain Orde the task of welcoming the stranger within their gates, they hurried with their explanations to their father; and it was by the hand of Sir George that Fairfax was conducted into the presence of their more formal aunt.

Still, though rendered presentable at the dinner-table by the friendly aid of Bob Orde, and encouraged by the General with all the soldierly cordiality of his nature, the young guest was evidently ill at ease. Notwithstanding the fragrant freshness of those lovely gardens, —— notwithstanding all the English comfort of the well-furnished villa, it was clear that he would have preferred his barrack-room at Z——, or the goatherd's hovel at Bocchetta !——

"The young man knows his place !"——was the comment of Aunt Martha, on finding herself alone with her nieces. "He is probably aware that he has no right to find himself in the circle of the governor's family."

"I cannot agree with you," cried Emma: "His tone is that of the best society. He has had a first-rate education. It is probably because he feels himself *superior* to the rest of the garrison at Z——, that he remains so secluded."

"Captain Fairfax is, I admit, a fine musician," observed Aunt Martha. "He took his part in those trios of Donizzetti's, at sight, in a style that surprised me. But perhaps he may have been brought up for the musical profession."

" I should scarcely think so, my dear aunt. He spoke of being slightly acquainted with my cousin,—of having dined at Harcourt Hall."—

" Well, my dear,—it is only too much the custom in England for people to invite fiddlers and singers to their tables."

" Captain Fairfax, I am convinced, was never intended for either a singer or a fiddler!" cried Emma, with indignation. " It is rather hard that one of the most gentlemanly officers in the garrison, because he shows less inclination than the rest to toady my father, and intrude into our privacy, should be judged with such severity!"

The consequence of this strenuous defence of the stranger on the part of her youngest niece was a perseverance in animosity on the part of the demure aunt. Pleased with the retiring manners of his guest, Sir George persisted that now they had got him at Santa

Chiara, he should not be let off so easily; and the wish of a governor being a command, particularly when expressed on the lawn of his own villa, there was nothing for it but to despatch a special messenger to ——— for his clothes, and pass the remainder of the week at Santa Chiara.

At the end of the week, indeed, poor Fairfax appeared to have lost his eagerness to get away. He was not only an adopted favourite with Sir George, but the two girls felt it so incumbent upon them to atone for the ungraciousness of the spinster aunt, by the kindness of their courtesies, that, shy as he was, the young stranger was beginning to feel himself thoroughly at home.

Bewitched by his noble horsemanship, old Robert took care he should be so well mounted as to put the fat aide-de-camp to the blush; and Emma Harcourt being fully justified in her surmise that Fairfax had received a superior education, the girls derived from his instructions in botanical and mineralogical science hints which induced them to pursue their neglected studies in natural history, so as to open a thousand sources of interest in the environs of the villa. Had not Orde been the best-natured of men, he must have felt mortified at being so completely eclipsed.

Aunt Martha, in short, was the only one of the family who still persisted in classing the hero of the wreck with the billiard-playing Ensign Browns and cigar-divan Lieutenant Smiths : and so efficacious is this sort of irrational opposition in forwarding an intimacy, that Sir George, little accustomed to be thwarted in such matters, became peremptory, and not only gave in her presence a general invitation to Fairfax (" a knife and fork always at my table at your service, and a bed under my roof"), but determined to offer him the aide-de-campship which the promised promotion of Captain Orde was shortly to leave vacant.

" The next thing, I make no doubt—the *very* next thing—we shall be having my brother offer him the hand of one of the girls, and her thirty thousand pounds !"—was the bitter cogitation of Aunt Martha. "A man of whom we know nothing——a man without fortune——without connexion——without——." Alas! there was no authenticated means of calculating his deficiencies!

Among them, however, could not certainly be numbered that charm of manner, that personal attraction, which is the surest letter of recommendation. Notwithstanding the favour in which he stood at the government-house, Arthur Fairfax was equally popular in his regiment. Throughout the garrison the hero of the wreck was a favourite.

Under these circumstances, it was scarcely likely that the two open-hearted girls, by whom he was admitted to terms of almost cousinly intimacy, should be more fastidious than the rest. But for the framed and glazed influence of Harcourt Hall, and the monthly arrival of the Debates, there is no saying to what extent of infidelity Sophia might have been tempted by the agreeable companionship of the new aide-de-camp.

But the heart of Emma surrendered at discretion; nay, Aunt Martha's prognostications were on a fair way towards being justified, —for Sir George, instead of appearing shocked at her undisguised predilection, often made it a subject of bantering during the absence of Fairfax.

Still, the young man himself hung back. The more encouraging towards him the deportment of the Harcourt family, the more diffident his reserve, the graver his deportment; and when it became no longer possible to mistake the intimation of the younger sister in his favour, he withdrew from their society as far as was compatible with the nature of his appointment. At Z—— he found such perpetual occupation for his time in duties that appeared to have altogether escaped the notice of his predecessor, as scarcely to leave him a moment's leisure.

As to Santa Chiara, he gradually ceased to set foot upon its delicious turf. Those charming shrubberies, combined with the influence of such a climate and such moonlight as perfected the spot, rendered the sojourn too dangerous. The fact was, that it was impossible to maintain the reserve he had imposed upon himself, amid the cordial domestic life of Santa Chiara.

It was, perhaps, on this account that Aunt Martha persisted in prolonging her sojourn there that autumn, till even the General began to find perpetual transit between his villa and the government-house bleak and tedious. Mild as are the winters of that genial island, there was no occasion to meet Christmas in the country, when the duties of Sir George Harcourt's position summoned him to the city ; and after repeated delays, the girls had at length the satisfaction of knowing that the day was fixed for their re-inauguration at the government-house.

The carnival was about to commence. Balls and rumours of balls were rife in the garrison ; and though Sophia bore the prospect of their renewed gaieties with suitable serenity, poor Emma could scarcely restrain her spirits to becoming decorum, as she reflected that, once more domesticated under the same roof with

Arthur Fairfax, he would be no longer able to assume a coldness where he had it not; and that the preference he had fully betrayed during their first six weeks of intimacy—the preference which fully sanctioned her own,—would again melt in his looks, and soften his manly voice.

"Whatever may be the motive of his recent reserve," thought the poor girl, "I may at least henceforward enjoy his society as a friend."

Even Sir George Harcourt, who had written home for the fullest particulars concerning the young man in whom he took so deep an interest the moment he determined on admitting him into his household, was delighted at the thoughts of having his little circle once more collected around him, enjoying the appropriate pleasures of their age.

"*To-morrow!*" whispered Emma to her sister, as they stood inspecting together the packing of their harp and piano, and the removal of their music-books, —— "to-morrow we shall be once more happy. Dearly as I love Santa Chiara, I long to find myself again on the old ramparts!——I will never again complain of the noise of the parade! The bay affords such a cheering prospect!"——

"And the Alcyone arrived yesterday," added Miss Harcourt. "Lord Algernon may have perhaps brought us letters from England, which he did not think it worth while to ride over here and deliver, as we were expected so soon."

"With *his* help, we might surely get up some tableaux or charades——as they did in the garrison the winter before our arrival!"—— observed Emma. "What they managed to do without *our* aid and that of Arthur Fairfax, they might certainly accomplish *now!*"

"Hush! here comes Aunt Martha, who seems to have taken an aversion to every thing like attempts at gaiety!"——whispered Miss Harcourt. "I am afraid she is come to scold us for our tardiness in packing!"

But no!——The frown upon the maidenly brow of the spinster was produced only by the inconsistency of her brother: who, after expressing so vehement a desire for their arrival at Z——, had just despatched an orderly with instructions for a counter-march! ——They were on no account to leave Santa Chiara till they heard further from him. He would ride over next day, or the day following, and explain his reasons.

Pre-assured that his "reasons" were excellent, the girls resigned themselves as patiently as they could to the delay. But, by the following evening, they had begun to discover that Santa Chiara, in its present dismantled state, was a most cheerless residence, and that the rainy season in Greece is as disagreeable as it is everywhere else. The bitterns screamed mournfully as they flew over the low roofs of the villa towards the marshes; and the dim sky was as dispiriting as their own state of suspense.

"Just like my brother!"——was the peevish ejaculation of Aunt Martha.

"So *un*like papa, on the contrary, that I am beginning to be almost alarmed!" was the murmured observation of Sophia to her

c 5

sister, when the middle of the second dreary day arrived, without bringing further orders, or an explanation of the preceding ones.

" This place was never intended for a winter residence. One has not a single comfort about one!"—said Mrs. Martha Harcourt, looking disdainfully at the cane-mats of the drawing-room, which a few juniper logs on the hearth were beginning to fill with smoke.

" But, dearest aunt, it was by your *own* express wish we remained here so long!"— returned Sophia.

" Certainly—so long as the fine weather lasted. But when once my brother had issued orders to break up the establishment, he might surely have known his own mind! I always determined to eat my Christmas dinner at Z——."

" And so you will!—We have still a week before us.—Depend upon it, we shall welcome in the new year by a merry dance at the government-house!"—

As Miss Harcourt uttered these words, the sound of horse's hoofs was heard in the court;

and in a moment the girls rushed to the hall-door to welcome their father. It was still daylight ; and both at the same moment perceived that his countenance was sad, and that he wore a crape round his hat.

" You have no bad news from England ! — My cousin Harcourt is well ?" cried Emma, perceiving that the sister was too much agitated to give utterance to the inquiry.

" Quite well ! I have had *no* news from England !" he replied, imprinting a kiss alternately on the foreheads of both, ere he advanced towards the drawing-room, on the threshold of which stood Aunt Martha, with an air of offended dignity ; and, to their great surprise, almost before he shook hands with her, the General, who was the most abstinent of men, asked for a glass of wine ! So tremulous, moreover, was the hand which raised it to his lips, that Emma discovered *his* agitation to be greater than even that of her sister. A sudden apprehension glanced into her mind ; but she had not breath to mention " the once loved name."

" You will perceive from my dress," said

the old soldier, his voice faltering with emotion, " that I have——that— But Sergeant Hanson probably warned you."

Emma now caught wildly hold of his arm, while Aunt Martha, alarmed in her turn, assured him that the orderly had merely delivered his letter, and galloped off. At the moment, Sir George Harcourt forgot that such had been his express orders.

" I fear then," said he, averting his face, and speaking more deliberately, " that I shall be the first to bring the ill news of poor Fairfax's untimely end.——I am come from attending his funeral."

Rightly had he judged that, since the worst *must* be known, it could not be told too abruptly ; the gradual enkindling and stifling of hope produced by over-cautious revelations being simply a prolongation of agony to the hearer. Nevertheless, the shock of the communication was stunning ; and while poor Emma remained stupified and exhausted by a series of fainting-fits, from which she was with difficulty recovered, her father proceeded to

unfold to Sophia and his sister the cruel particulars of an event which even the severe
spinster consecrated by her tears.

"The poor lad was sacrificed," said Sir
George, "absolutely sacrificed—I am afraid
that, as the world contemplates such matters,
there was no help for it; but, in the eyes of
common sense and Christian principle, poor
Fairfax might as well have had his throat cut!"

"A duel, then?"—demanded Sophia, in a
subdued voice.

"A duel."

"And could not the interference of seconds—"

"No, my dear!—Had I myself been one of
them, I should have said that he must fight.
The circumstances were very peculiar. The
quarrel arose from an accusation of cowar-
dice,—of a duel evaded,—which—. But it
is a long story, of which, at present, I can
tell you only that, on the day of the arrival
of the Alcyone, when Lord Algernon caught
sight of Fairfax for the first time, he foolishly
exclaimed, 'What *that* fellow in the ——th?
I thought he had been forced to leave the

army ?'   The brother officers of poor Fairfax
of course insisted on an explanation, which,
on finding what a storm he had raised by his
chattering, Lord Algernon positively refused.
One or two of those officers of the garrison,
however, who have shown jealousy of Fairfax's rapid advancement, took care that the
story should reach his ears, and *his* demand
for an explanation from Lord Algernon was
not of course to be denied like the rest.   He-
berden took him the message.   The answer
consisted in the haughty taunt of ' Tell Captain
Fairfax I had the honour to visit Bermuda
shortly after his retirement from the—5th !' "

" There *was* some foundation then for the
contemptuous observations of Lord Algernon ?"——inquired Aunt Martha, eagerly.

" You shall hear, my dear sister,——give me
time, and you shall hear.   Foundation or no
foundation, Fairfax conducted himself in such
a manner towards Lord Algernon within an
hour of receiving his message, that a meeting
was indispensable !"

" Indispensable ?"——murmured Sophia Harcourt, whose tears were now falling unrestrainedly.

" Though I can assure you that Lord Algernon made a *concession* of *accepting* poor Fairfax's challenge ! ' Under all the circumstances, I feel that I should be justified in refusing,' said he.   ' But *I* am not the fellow to skulk out of an affair provoked by my own rashness ;   and, from all I have heard of Captain Fairfax during the last four-and-twenty hours, shall not be sorry, if the opportunity avails, to restore him to the position in public estimation which, for his own sake, I trust he has unjustly forfeited.' "

" A wondrous act of kindness, certainly !" cried Sophia, bitterly.

" It *was*, my dear, I promise you, in a professional point of view.   According to poor Fairfax's death-bed avowals to me, few could have blamed Lord Algernon for refusing to go out with him.   For Fairfax, though as brave a fellow as ever trod the earth, had incurred a fatal imputation !   Poor lad, poor lad !——He went through tortures during the

seven hours he survived his wound !"——faltered
Sir George. " He—he was carried to the
hospital. It was there I visited him.——It was
there he relieved his mind by delivering to
me a written explanation, which he had prepared previous to the meeting.——Doubtless it
was some comfort to him that I was able,
after perusing it, to shake him by the hand
with greater affection than ever.——I told him
I could not wish a son of my own to have
acted otherwise !——Poor fellow !——I believe it
was a comfort to him to hear as much!——and
I closed his eyes with the less heaviness of
heart for having afforded it. But the world
does not deal tenderly with such matters ; and
I am sadly afraid that, by the many to whom
it is impossible to communicate Arthur Fairfax's justification, his name may still come to
be harshly dealt with, and myself to be
severely handled for the tenderness I have
shown towards his memory !"

It was some time before Sophia could absent herself sufficiently long from the bedside
of her sister to entreat from her father the

further explanations she was unwilling to ask in presence of one so ill inclined towards him, who was gone from among them, as her aunt. She was, however, too well aware of the necessity of being able to meet the interrogations of poor Emma with more consolatory intelligence than she had yet to give, not to seek the first occasion of being alone with Sir George.

" I see my fears had not outstripped the truth, Sophy ! "—said he.   The affections of my poor girl *were* given to this noble fellow ! —What shall we—what *can* we do to comfort her ?—She must not, at present, go back to Z——.   His death-bed is *there*,—his grave is *there*; and though the sympathies of the whole garrison are enlisted on his side, I should be sorry that the state of her feelings became a matter of publicity.   I have, therefore, desired my sister to prepare for spending the winter here.   I have ordered every thing to be replaced in its usual state.—As soon as the spring breaks, we will travel—we will visit the Morea."——

" Alas ! my dear father, considering the

delight with which *he* used to contemplate joining us in that very expedition, and the number of times that Emma and he have traced it out together, I fear such a tour would do more harm than good."

" We will go to England, then; anywhere —*anywhere* likely to restore my poor dear child to herself!—For my sister was right, Sophy; after all, my sister was right.—There was no excuse for my throwing a handsome young fellow so much into your society, of whose antecedent life I knew so little."

It was not likely that Sir George's self-accusations would be lessened on perceiving in the sequel, by the calm desperation of poor Emma's grief, how far more serious than he supposed was her ill-starred passion! The rapidly conceived attachments of very young persons are only too apt to strike thus deeply into the virgin soil of the heart. Had time been allowed, sunshine and prosperity might have dwindled its growth. But misfortune seemed to have consecrated it for ever—perpetuated it as with the changelessness of marble.

"All is over for me, father!" murmured the heart-broken girl, in reply to his exhortations. "Tell me only how he died, and that his grave is not dishonoured in your eyes!"

While the General devoted himself to upraising this broken reed, Sophia hastened to acquaint herself with the details contained in the papers committed by Arthur Fairfax to her father.

"Aware that disastrous circumstances, aided by my own inexperience of the world, have exposed me to obloquy," wrote the unfortunate young man, "I prepare myself for the fate—I will not say *awaiting* me,—but the fate I am about to seek—by enabling the few whom I would fain interest in my memory, to judge with leniency the perplexities of my brief career.

"I am the only surviving son of the late Admiral Sir Arthur Fairfax. My mother having married again shortly after his death, I was educated in the family of my guardian —a clergyman,—a distant kinsman,—whose affection more than supplied the parent I had lost.——Inheriting from the Admiral a fortune of twenty thousand pounds, Mr. Otway judged it expedient that, previous to entering the army, which I had selected as my profession, I should pass a few years at Sandhurst; and it was only during my vacations that I was a member of his family circle.

" It was perhaps because that family consisted of two daughters, nearly of my own age, that, as I advanced to manhood, he so strongly insisted on the necessity of a military education. For though he loved me as a son, and, I am convinced, desired nothing more earnestly than that I should bestow my heart and hand on one of his girls, he was too conscientious a man not to feel that it became him, as my guardian, to prevent my entangling myself in an engagement till I had seen more of the world. He might have spared himself all uneasiness !——Young people brought up so familiarly together as I had been with Mary and Lucy, seldom fall in love. The girls were to me as dear sisters,——dearer perhaps than *real* sisters, from the circumstance of the reserves produced by want of kindred; and when, at the early age of seventeen, Mary Otway fell a victim to a malignant fever, caught in administering aid to one of her father's parishioners, I doubt whether even her father or her heartbroken sister lamented her more fondly than myself.

"Now, however, that Lucy was left alone, there was additional motive for objecting to me as an inmate at Hartstonge Vicarage; and it was the consciousness of this that determined me to accept a proposal made to me, previous to the last vacation I was to spend at Sandhurst, by one of my brother cadets, the eldest son of an Irish baronet, to join him in an excursion to the Lakes.—It was arranged that we should proceed together to Westmoreland; but the consent of Mr. Otway being indispensable to our project, Pakenham was to accompany me for a few days to Hartstonge.

"In those few days, he became so captivated by poor Lucy's beauty and simplicity of character, as to contrive the postponement of our tour; and so well did he recommend himself to the hospitable vicar and his daughter, that an invitation to prolong his stay was a matter of course. In short, he remained till he had won the confidence of the one and the affections of the other. As there wanted a year to the completion of his majority (till when it was useless, he thought, to provoke the interference of his father), he prevailed on Miss Otway to content herself with a clandestine engagement; and the good vicar, who was any thing but a man of the world, regarded his departure without uneasiness, entreating him to visit Hartstonge again as soon as he should obtain his commission.

" In the interim I obtained mine; and it was on taking leave of me, when I quitted the vicarage to join my regiment at Cork, that the old man, in addition to his earnest and affectionate exhortations, and in a spirit of prescience not unusual to those whose days are numbered, adjured me, when I gratefully acknowledged the care with which he had watched over my boyhood, to promise him that should Lucy, at some future time, stand in need of protection, I would be unto her as a brother.

" ' I once entertained hopes,' said he, with tears in his eyes, ' that a closer bond might unite you. But this desire, my dear Arthur, is frustrated; Lucy has admitted to me that her heart is engaged. If, therefore, my dear boy, either in her single or married life, you behold her exposed to dangers such as are apt to beset the woman lacking better guardianship than a feeble arm like mine, remember her old father's gray hairs and loving kindness towards you; and take part with her as if indeed my son.'

" My reply was all he could desire; and when, ere twelvemonths elapsed, I learned, in a distant garrison, that Pakenham, though still a minor, had persuaded the imprudent Lucy to elope with him, and that this rash step had been succeeded within a few weeks by the death of her excellent father, a painful presentiment forewarned me of the likelihood that I might be only too speedily called upon for the performance of my promise.

" For, during the opportunities of that accidental visit to Hartstonge, having had occasion to see my schoolfellow in a new and more intimate light, I had discovered much to dislike in him,——more to disapprove ;——so much, indeed, that already I had exercised my brotherly privileges with Lucy, by imploring her to examine her own heart and *his* right carefully, ere she was induced to fulfil her engagement.

" But she was eighteen, and, for the first time, passionately beloved.——I had no right to feel surprised on hearing of her marriage !——

" My letters of congratulation and condolence remained unanswered ; as I afterwards learned, from having fallen into the hands of Pakenham, who was little inclined that my office of brotherly service should reach his wife.   Conceiving, therefore, that Lucy, recognized by her husband's family, stood in no need of my aid, I addressed myself to my professional duties without further anxiety on her account ; and being now in the enjoyment of a liberal income, found my expectations of happiness fully answered. Eager to obtain promotion, I made no attempt to quit my regiment when it was ordered to the West Indies. A soldier at heart, I had no desire to evade the minor hazards of my profession.

" I had been three months in garrison at Bermuda, enjoying the personal consideration derivable from excellent letters of recommendation to the governor and leading personages of the colony, when, one morning, I was roused by my servant with the pleasing intelligence that the English packet was arrived, and the astounding news that it had brought over ' my sister.'

" ' You are mistaken, Peter,' said I; ' strangely mistaken !' and I was about to add that I possessed neither brother nor sister, when he placed a letter in my hand, stating that it came from ' my sister, Mrs. Otway ;' and that she and ' the child' were waiting for me at the hotel.

" Beyond measure startled by the intelligence, I hastened to poor Lucy, almost without giving myself time to master the melancholy contents of her letter.

" ' I have been deceived and betrayed,' was all I could hastily decipher. ' My marriage proves to be invalid. Edward has cast us off—me and my unfortunate boy—after dissipating all that was left me by my father. My hope, dear Arthur, is in *you*—in my adopted brother! But lest the world should regard such a tie with suspicion, I have announced myself in the packet as your sister. *Do* not gainsay me—*do* not expose me to shame!'——

" The consequence of a hasty perusal of this appeal to my feelings was that, on rushing to the shore to welcome the unfortunate wanderer, I inquired, according to her desire, for ' my sister, Mrs. Otway;' and the arrival of so near a relative having transpired, in the course of the ensuing day, every lady in the colony with whom I was acquainted called upon us with offers of hospitality and kindness.

" Then it was I discovered the danger of

the step I had taken!——For though careful to instal Lucy and her poor boy in my comfortable private house, while I removed to barracks, expressly to avoid any future misinterpretation of our relative position and sentiments, still, I *had* introduced her as my sister to those in whom I had not sufficient confidence to relate the unhappy story of her wrongs.

" My first movement in her behalf was to engage the best legal advice in England, to ascertain how far the legality of her marriage could be established. They gave me no hope. Pakenham had turned out a villain; and there was no chance of legitimatizing her child—— no chance of redeeming herself from the miseries of her degradation.——Poor Lucy!—— It was a sad trial to be a constant witness of her repinings. For she loved him still, the origin of her misfortunes; and so thoroughly were her feelings towards me at variance with any tender sentiment, and so often was she disposed to resent the harshness of my remarks upon Pakenham's conduct, that I overlooked even the possibility of our intimacy becoming a matter of blame, in the event of our secret being discovered. We liked each other less than when living together at Hartstonge ; and nothing but gratitude and dependence on *her* part, and a sense of duty on mine, served to prolong the false position which a moment of imprudence had created.

" It was decided that the following spring she should return to England ; and though it was her eager desire to increase, by her own industry, the aid I was enabled to afford my adopted sister, I had secretly determined to frustrate her projects. I was to accompany her to England, and return in the course of a month or two. For poor Lucy, enfeebled by affliction and a trying climate, was in no situation to take care of herself.

" ' I have no friend on earth but *you*, Arthur !' was her constant exclamation. ' My child has no friend but *you !*—What would become of us both, were we to lose you ; and how fervently, if my father be per-

mitted to look down from heaven, must he
bless you for your noble redemption of your
promise !'——

"By such tender appeals, I was bound a
slave to her cause. On quitting Bermuda, I
acknowledged, as an affectionate brother might
have done, the kindnesses heaped upon Mrs.
Otway and her child by my Creole friends.
A thousand comforts were by their interposition provided for her on the voyage ; and they
took leave of us both, anticipating my speedy
return.

"On arriving in England, however, the
health of my poor nominal sister had become
still more precarious ; and the dread of leaving her to die alone, bequeathing her unpro-
tected child to the mercies of strangers,
determined me to quit my regiment.

"I did so. I went on half-pay. I attended,
as a brother, that ill-starred and dying
woman. But long before I laid her in the
grave, I found that, at Bermuda, all had
transpired ! Apprised of the fraud we had
perpetrated upon their good faith, the angry

Bermudians indulged in the most cruel accusations,—nay, Lucy was stated to have been my mistress, and Pakenham's child my own !———

" Had I pursued my original intention of returning to the colony, I should probably have been made accountable for my imprudence, by more than one indignant father and husband, who believed that I had imposed a worthless woman upon their hospitality ; and when they saw me gazetted out of the regiment, no one entertained a doubt that I had slunk from the just vengeance of my traducers !——

" Not a syllable of all this, however, at that period reached my ears. Lucy was dying, dying slowly, and of a broken heart ;——and in the seclusion of our quiet residence on the southern coast, not an angry whisper was allowed to disturb the tranquillity of the expiring sufferer.

She survived, alas ! just long enough to perceive that, either by inheritance or contagion, the germ of pulmonary disease was be-

coming developed in her more than orphan
boy; and her last words conveyed as solemn
a bequeathment of the poor little fellow to
my parental care, as the adjuration of her
father had originally intrusted *her*.

" And thus, in the dawn of life, I became
fettered by the ties, without the joys, of wed-
lock and paternity; and, absorbed in the
duties they conveyed, remained ignorant of
the stigma conveyed by the discovery of my
involuntary falsehood, and hasty retreat from
my regiment. I knew *nothing* of all that had
occurred, till it was too late! On my word,
as a man of honour and a gentleman, I knew
nothing of it; and my first impression on
discovering the evil opinions connected with
my name was to hasten back to Bermuda,
and fix a quarrel on any man who might feel
inclined to persist in his resentments.——But
what a return for the hospitalities I had received;——I being manifestly in the wrong!

" My next determination,—after ascertaining that no report of what had only been
whispered at Bermuda had been made to the

Horse-guards by my commanding officer, who was only acquainted with the rumours to my prejudice after I had quitted the regiment,— was to resume my professional career; and, if possible, reconquer the golden opinions of which no real act of turpitude had deprived me.

" Such were the circumstances under which I landed at Z———; and in recalling to mind the beneficent indulgence with which my attempts were received, I seem to feel with new and more insupportable bitterness the present fatal interruption.

" A thousand times have I been on the point of revealing my painful secret to Sir George Harcourt; a thousand times of attempting to find courage for an explanation with his lovely daughter.—What I have endured of anxiety and self-accusation, no mortal can conceive. I knew the basis of my unparalleled happiness to be tottering.—Any hour—any moment — might precipitate me from the height of human felicity into obloquy and despair !——

" Nor can I blame Lord Algernon for the part he has taken: 'Judge not that ye be not judged,' is a canon of Christian law which few of us are scrupulous to practise, and appearances were grievously against me.

" Fortune is against me too!—A stain is upon my character, which nothing but blood —either my own or my adversary's—can efface.—I must become a murderer or a victim!"——

" Nor yet the only victim," mused Sophia Harcourt, when, with tearful eyes, she reached the close of this afflicting narrative.   " This kind-hearted and ill-starred being has carried with him to his untimely grave the peace of mind of my poor sister!"

*   *   *   *   *   *

The little colony of Z—— has now become one of the most cheerless of the Mediterranean.   Though still endowed with the valuable public works and institutions created under the command of Sir George Harcourt, the garrison has never recovered the cloud produced by the mournful events originating in his resignation of the government; and his successor, a strict disciplinarian, and dry calculating Scotsman, finds it impossible to contend against the prejudices of popularity connected with the favourite name. In *his* well-ordered official household, there is a total absence of the kindly family feeling which prevailed from the Harcourts. Last winter, there were no private theatricals in the garrison; last autumn, not a yacht dropped anchor in the bay.

If the mind of poor Sir George were still open to pleasurable impressions, he might derive some solace, in the afflictions of his old age, from knowing how truly his memory is held in respect in the little colony almost founded under his administration. But at Harcourt Hall (where, since the death of his sister, he has resided with his surviving daughter Sophia, and her husband) the name of Z—— is never mentioned. For in the garrison chapel of that island of the dark blue waters lie the remains of her whose loss has saddened the days of the happy family;

the devoted girl who survived only a few weeks the object of her first affection, and made it her death-bed request that she might be interred in the same spot with him whose head the General had laid in the grave.

Her last wish was faithfully accomplished. The population of the whole island accompanied to her last resting-place the gentle being whose life had been a life of charity and love. Flowers from thousands of rude but honest hands were flung upon the coffin of the governor's daughter; and to those who, deceived by its former good renown as an agreeable residence, are still tempted to visit the island, a marble slab is pointed out as serving for a memorial of the unfortunate pair, on which, by the express desire of Emma, is inscribed the memorable sentence cited by the victim of a false impression and calumnious report—

" JUDGE NOT, THAT YE BE NOT JUDGED !"

A PASSAGE IN THE CIVIL WARS.

" What, *more* novels ?" cried my old aunt
Barbara, examining through her spectacles
the title of a new work I was rash or dutiful
enough to lay before her ; " will you never
attempt something useful, something likely to
last ?——All this frippery, the growth of a day,
will never survive to a morrow. —— Jonah's
gourd, child, Jonah's gourd.——Truth is the
rock of ages, and a single fact worth a thousand fictions.   If you must needs scribble, why
not history, which, if it did not amuse, might
at least edify ?"

I ventured, in a low voice, to suggest the
retort of Sir Robert Walpole to his son
Horace, when he proposed reading some historical work for the diversion of his hours of
sickness :——"Anything you please but history.
That *must* be lies."

"At all events," remonstrated the old lady, " if you choose to invent, if not *vrai*, be *vrai-semblable.* You novelists of the day, who treat of other times and countries, costume your characters over head and ears, in order to afford what is called local colouring. The manner and not the matter is all you care for. Mere poverty of invention ! When you want to bring Charles II. or Henri IV. before your readers, it must be ' Odd's fish,' or ' *Ventre Saint Gris*,' in every line ; and the quantity of velvet and Venice point, ruffs and trunk-hose, introduced to fill out your pages might furnish the property-room of a theatre. And if hoops, rouge, patches, lapdogs, and Mare-chale powder, go three parts of the way to make out a tale of the time of Louis XV., your grandchildren, I suppose, will have to record anecdotes of their ancestors, in which crinolines and Chesterfield-wrappers play the leading parts."

"But how, my dear madam," said I, "would you convey a graphic notion of the manners of the day without such accessories? We know

that, in the days of James I., the nether garments of the Lords and Commons were expanded into such rotundity, by paddings of
horsehair or bran, that the seats of the Houses
of Parliament had to be enlarged for their
accommodation ; and posterity will be sure to
adduce, among the causes of desertion of the
public boxes of our theatres, the impossibility
of introducing into them the superabundance
of petticoats constituting the mode of the
day : these traits, consequently, become historical."

"I grant you ! But let them be kept subor-
dinate. Why should they be supposed to give
a colouring to the times we live in ? —— The
grave lies of history, to which Walpole ad-
verted, are sure to be detected and pointed
out by succeeding historians. But nobody
is at the trouble of measuring the exaggera-
tions of the novelist ; and his colouring, however false, is accepted as true to the hour.
If Lady Mary Wortley Montagu's letters
to her sister had never seen the light, pointing
out the vulgarity of Richardson's sketches of

high life (of which, as a contemporary, a duke's daughter and a woman of discernment, she was a sufficient judge), we should continue to ascribe to Lovelace the manners of a man of supreme fashion of his day, and to see in Lady G—— an exquisite woman of quality !"

Of what avail to point out to the old lady that these life-like inventions are something more and something better than mere fac-similes !

"Look here, child," continued she, opening an old tortoiseshell casket, which she had fetched while speaking from one of her favourite hoards, and which, when opened, emitted a powerful scent of amber and musk. "Here are the letters of the beautiful Marchioness of G——, afterwards Duchess of R——, to my sister, containing the chitchat and scandal of her day, related in the simple style in which one woman of her condition is accustomed to write to another. Here is her note, inviting your poor dear aunt to accompany her to the first representation of the 'School for Scandal,' in company with two boon companions of the Prince of Wales, who have since become historical. After perusing this correspondence, you will laugh at the over-written descriptions, in modern novels, of those Pantheon and Ranelagh days!"

I was in hopes my aunt Barbara was about to offer this interesting collection to my perusal. But she thought better of it.

" These," said she, " are sacred, as family relics of the dearest of sisters. But, trust me, there is scarcely a considerable family in the realm which does not possess trunks full of epistolary treasures. At the death of his wife, a man is apt to set aside her confidential papers, either from personal regard, or for future examination. The leisure day for this never arrives. They are bequeathed from father to son, from son to grandson. The ink waxes pale, the paper mildewed. In the fourth generation they have grown too damp to burn, and decipherable only by the curious eye of the antiquarian or genealogist. I could myself point out to you dozens of families rich in similar treasures, who would be rather proud than reluctant to submit them to publication."

"Point them out then, my dear madam, in all charity!" was of course the answer; "or, if possible, extend your kindness by procuring me access to such archives."

"I will do my best," replied the old lady; "but it is never safe to answer for other people. I could, however, *tell* you heaps of stories far more striking than I have seen of late in print, legendary either in our own family or those of my friends. I need not remind you, that, being orphans, I and my two sisters were educated by our excellent grandmother, who died during the riots of '80, in the full enjoyment of her faculties, though seven years older than the eighteenth century. Born in Queen Mary's time, and a shrewd observer of men and things, a world of anecdotes enriched her memory, which would probably remain in mine, but for the still more vivid reminiscences of my own more stirring times."

"Still," said I, eager to ascertain by a

specimen the value of these family legends, " a few of them must sometimes recur to you, as worthy of narration ?"

" An anecdote glanced into my mind just now," said my aunt Barbara, " suggested by the faded miniature of my poor sister, which met my eye on opening yonder casket."

Proper curiosity having been avowed on my part, the old lady proceeded to relate her story; tediously enough, for she could not refrain from interlarding her narrative with moral reflections, somewhat of the tritest. On the whole, however, it struck me as likely to excite the interest of the public.

———

Towards the end of the reign of Charles II., then, there resided in an old manor-house, on the borders of Kent, a well-descended family of the name of Hillenfield :——people not sufficiently near the foot of the throne to render it incumbent on them to take an active part in the civil war; or to revel in the joys of the licentious reign by which peace was succeeded.

They lived upon their lands, finding sufficient pleasure in their cultivation and prosperity from the result; inclining towards the
grave in matters of religion, and towards the
sober in matters of conviviality; yet loved
and respected among their neighbours, as
charitable to the poor, and hospitable, after
their own notions, to the rich.

Nevertheless, though the Hillenfields had
refrained from court and even city, during
those days of despotic prodigality which have
reached our own under such glaring colours
only because they had the witty Hamilton for
their chronicler, and two or three bars sinis-
ter to bequeath to our peerage, through the
progeny of royal concubines, the old manor-
house of Hillenfield was beginning to assume
a somewhat more worldly hue, in honour of
an only daughter growing up into heiresshood
under its roof.

Monica Hillenfield, independent of the
fourteen hundred per annum to descend to her
(a large fortune in those days), was a very
lovely creature, as one of the finest pictures

of Kneller, painted in her maturity, survives
to attest; an accomplished maiden, moreover,
as you may guess from the fine Italian hand
in the early pages of your grandmother's
recipe-book, while the famous verses of Prior,
addressed to " Mistress Monica Hillenfield
playing upon the lute," render extravagant
honours to her musical talents.

Certain it is that, from the day Monica
attained the age of sixteen, a lovely rose
seemed to have blossomed among the old
yew-trees of the Manor-gardens. Though
the roads of the neighbourhood were none of
the best, visitors now hastened from all quar-
ters to pay their devoirs to the Hillenfields;
and neither Knowle nor Penshurst, neither
Hever nor Summerhill, with all their splendours and works of art, had half the attraction of that quaint old grange, with its par-
lours of carved wainscot and paved dining-
hall.

Monica was a gay-hearted creature, considering the somewhat formal sobrieties of her
parentage. Her white teeth were constantly

visible between her parted lips, and her blue
eyes brought gladness with them, like the
flowers among the corn. The grace of her
deportment was wholly of Nature's bestowing.
Every gesture was untutored; but her smiles
and tears, and, above all, her blushes, lay so
near the surface, that those who looked upon
her found no leisure to ascertain whether her
curtsey might not be more dignified, or whether she were qualified to hold her own among
the accomplished beauties of Whitehall.

On that point, however, one of her father's
neighbours entertained no doubt. Sir Gervase de Bellyn (whose ancestral residence of
Marks Castle stood within a few miles of the
Manor,) had already signified to his only son
that he could not do better than make their
hands, hearts, and estates, one and indivisible,
so soon as Monica should attain her eighteenth
year and sufficient discretion to represent the
family honours at the court of the new king,
of whom all the good was predicted, usually
discerned at the commencement of every
reign.

"You have a great part to play in the world," said Sir Gervase to his tall, grave, reserved son, "and will play it none the worse for an early and prosperous marriage. As soon as your age permits, you will be returned to Parliament for the Shire, which my infirm health no longer permits me to represent; when it will be a comfort to me, my dear son, to know you secured against the temptations of the great Babylon, by the safeguard of a lovely and loving partner for life."

In reply, Hugh de Bellyn bowed low and submissively; and in truth there was nothing in the prospect of a gratuitous seat in Parliament, and a wife rich in all the best endowments of this world, to provoke opposition to the will of his father. But having every reason to believe his suit would be unsuccessful, he took upon himself to declare there was somewhat more of giddiness in the temper and deportment of young Mistress Hillenfield than squared with his notions of decorum.

"I grant you,—I grant you," cried Sir

Gervase, " were she other than a child. Nor should I have felt altogether content at seeing you appear at the court of our late sovereign with a bride so attractive, and so little of an age or character to defy admiration. But times are altered at Whitehall. The queen has other thoughts in her mind than to encourage the pranks which, in Charles's time, exceeded all bounds of discretion."

" Nevertheless," persisted Hugh de Bellyn, " there is a waywardness about Mr. Hillenfield's daughter which leads me to infer that no choice but her own will be exercised in the matter of her marriage."

" And why, pray, should not her choice fall upon yourself?" cried his father, out of all patience. " Is she likely to chance upon a youth of fairer inches, of purer descent, or less encumbered estate? I hold her a lucky wench to have within her reach a match so more than proportioned to her merits; a match that would fix her in an honourable position of life, without going further in search of it than the paling of her father's paddock."

Not to stand disputing with the parent he
was bound to reverence, Hugh de Bellyn
thought it advisable to remember that the
keepers were waiting for him to repair to the
decoy. He did not care to admit that already
the lovely Monica had shown pointed disre-
spect to his attentions ; and that, whenever
the backs of the Squire and Mrs. Hillenfield
were turned, she took no pains to disguise her
good understanding with a handsome young
standard-bearer of the King's guard, a cousin
of the Penshurst family, who occasionally
visited in the neighbourhood.

To have admitted his courtship before their
faces, had been utterly unavailing. For
young Clifford was a cadet and a Catholic,
with no patrimony but his sword, born of a
race of Cavaliers, and spendthrift parents ;—
the last man on earth to suit the sober views of
the Hillenfields for their only child. The young
couple were consequently forced to content
themselves with hope—a far-off hope—that
the King's favour and promotion might some
day or other justify his aspiring to her hand.

Hearts of sixteen and twenty are easily kept in cheer by such visions. The buoyant atmosphere of youth bears nutriment in itself; and the young couple had already accustomed themselves to meet and part, and part and meet again, with tears in their eyes, through which their sunny smiles shone only the brighter.

Each trusted wholly in the other. Monica had no fears of the rival influence of the lovely ladies of the Court, nor Arthur of the authority of the old people in favour of some worthier pretendant to her affections. Absent or present, they belonged to each other. They had said it— they had sworn it,—amid the junketing of more than one Christmas revel, amid the silence of more than one secret meeting in the woods of Hillenfield; nor was Hugh de Bellyn the only one of their neighbours who took note of their clandestine wooing.

At length, the two allotted years having elapsed, Sir Gervase, without a word of further warning to his son, set forth one day

in the coach and six which had scarcely seen
the light since the decease of the late Lady de
Bellyn, to make formal proposals to the
Hillenfields for the hand of their daughter.
On arriving at the Manor, Monica having accompanied her father in an afternoon ramble
on her pacing nag, he found the Squire's lady
dozing in her easy chair, while the old
chaplain was drowsily reciting the evening
service, which had an infallibly sedative effect
upon her nerves.   The flattering overtures of
her visitor, however, commanded instant attention ; and, before she had half expressed
her satisfaction in the prospect of so happy
an alliance, Mr. Hillenfield returned, and,
Monica having been despatched to her own
apartment, the proposition was renewed and
as graciously received. by the father as by the
less authoritative parent.

Of the assent of the young people nothing
was said.   In those days it was a matter of
course that children should obey their parents,
and the Hillenfields as little doubted that
Monica would thankfully accept any partner

of their proposing, as that their neighbour of Mark's Castle was acting with the full privity of his son.

So little indeed did they mistrust the passive obedience of a daughter so lately a child, that it occurred to them as a part of their parental duty to afford her a somewhat more extended glimpse of the world, before they presented to her the man they had fixed upon as her husband. They had long projected a month's sojourn in the metropolis, from which their estate was distant only a morning's journey; and, though the misguidance of James had already overclouded the prospects and pleasures of the Court, so that there was no longer delight for persons of grave persuasions like the Hillenfields, they had kinsfolk well settled in London, by whose aid they might obtain a glimpse of the pastimes of the town, without comprising themselves among the papists and foreign adventurers enjoying the full tide of royal favour at Whitehall.

This journey proved a sad vexation to old

De Bellyn, who considered it an undue stretch
of parental condescension; and contented
himself with wishing them a pleasant journey
and safe return; promising to abide, till then,
their answer to his suit.   But the joy of
Monica at so sudden a change in her monoto-
nous existence knew no bounds.   Her arms
were alternately round the neck of father
and mother.   One moment she was upon her
knees before the old Squire, interrogating him
concerning all he remembered of London in
his days of Clement's Inn, (the London of
the Commonwealth, not the London of the
Stuarts); the next, she was hurrying their
dilatory old waiting-woman, to whom a
journey to London was as a journey to Ispa-
han.   Of her real motive for joy, Monica of
course said nothing.   It was only in the
secrecy of her own heart that she rejoiced at
the prospect of startling her dear Arthur, by
suddenly pouncing upon him amid his pleasures.

By a singular chance, Clifford's was the
first familiar face they beheld after entering

London!—As their cumbrous coach made its way along the narrow street leading from Westminster to Whitehall, they were loudly called upon to make way for the king's equipage; preceding which, with his sword and cuirass glistening in the sun, and his gallant shoulder-knot and gauntlets speckless as snow, rode Arthur Clifford, reining a highly-managed horse with practised grace and adroitness.

In a moment, all the blood in Monica's frame was concentered in her heart, leaving her cheeks of ashy paleness. But so naturally did the old people ascribe the emotions of their loyal child to the first aspect of her sovereign, that she was not even called upon to account for her sudden faintness.

The young soldier to whom they had so often and cordially afforded country hospitality, being thus happily apprized of their arrival in the capital, was soon at their house, with offers of his services, whenever released from attendance on his royal master; and he accordingly not only accompanied them from

Hall to Abbey, from the Abbey to the White
Tower, from the Tower to Guildhall, but pro-
cured them admittance into the Banqueting
Hall, to witness one of the galas of the
Court.

To the playhouse, it accorded not with the
strictness of their ideas to resort. But whenever they walked forth for air into the King's
Park, nothing seemed more fitting than that
the young guardsman should place himself by
the side of their fair daughter, as guardian
and protector; for, though masked and
hooded, something in the sprightliness of her
step and airiness of her figure was sure to at-
tract attention.

Amid a hundred novel pleasures, the appointed time of their sojourn wore rapidly
away, while Mrs. Hillenfield was extending
her purchases of woman's gear in all directions, with a view to the wedding that was
to follow their return to the Manor. But,
above all, without apprizing Monica of the
object of the measure, her father chose that
she should sit for her portrait to a rare Italian

enameller, who had accompanied the queen from Modena; access to whose works was procured for them by Clifford's intermediation.

"It will be a choice gift for the old knight!" observed Mr. Hillenfield to his wife, while settling between them that Monica's dress should be a tunic of white taffeta, with her hair falling in natural ringlets on either side of her face. But to whomever destined, a lovely portrait it was; and Monica and Clifford admired it even more than the old people, for the slowness of its progress was the cause of delaying the return of the family into Kent.

Better, however, had they gone at the precise moment fixed! For the longer they stayed, the more was the old high-churchman disgusted at the aspect of public affairs; and many a rough argument occurred betwixt him and Arthur respecting the legality of the king's proceedings, and the consequences to be apprehended from his barefaced disregard to the terms of settlement, under which his brother had been replaced on the throne.

Arthur Clifford, of course, spoke as he felt ; and felt as the king's faithful servant, soldier, and fellow-Catholic might be expected to feel. Nor could even the silent chidings of Monica's deep blue eyes repress the ebullitions of his anger, when the old people declared that the rash monarch would certainly lose his crown, and deserved to lose his head !——

He began almost to wish them home again, that the blood might cease to boil in his veins. Though he pressed the hand of his own Monica more fondly than ever at parting, he could not refrain from cursing the destiny which had made her the child of parents so circumscribed in policy and faith.

On the other hand, as they journeyed back towards the Manor, the old people thought only of the joy they were about to create at Mark's Castle. They mentioned Arthur's name only to add (in acknowledging his good service as a cicerone) that it was no wonder he should be so astray in political and religious faith : his mother having died deranged, and his elder brother being occasionally afflicted with the same terrible malady.

But Monica listened unmoved; convinced that her parents had discovered her predilection, and were seeking to disgust her with the object of her imprudent choice. Because he had neither houses nor lands, they chose to heap on the shoulders of Arthur every defect they could imagine.

Meanwhile the re-assurances conveyed to Mark's Castle by Mr. Hillenfield, produced all the anticipated results. Hugh de Bellyn was half out of his wits with surprise and joy.

" I little expected such good fortune!" said the grave young man; " I fancied her heart was otherwise disposed of. Thanks be to Heaven, she is wiser than I wot of!— Thanks be to Heaven, she has seen the folly of her early choice !"

On the morrow, he set forth to accompany his father to the Manor, in the joyous expectation of finding her blue eyes turned for the first time with favour upon himself; and never had the wild blossoms of the hedgerows appeared to him so fragrant, or the fields of purple clover so vivid, or the blue sky over all so cheering, as now, that he was about to secure a gentle partner to whose sympathy he might point out their attraction.

But, alas! there met them by the way an express, wearing the livery of the Hillenfields, entreating them, for a time, to postpone their visit, the young lady of the Manor having fallen into sudden sickness. A fit of passion, on learning that her destinies had been surreptitiously disposed of, had betrayed all to her parents.

While Monica was weeping and wringing her hands, and the old people were raging and storming against each other's blindness, in having, for six weeks past, thrown the lovers perpetually together, Sir Gervase and his son returned home disconsolately to the Castle. But, alas! before they had time to marvel about the matter, tidings of still deeper import were circulated through the country.

The deposition of the king, and an invitation to his Protestant son-in-law, already substantiated the predictions of old Hillenfield.

The hearts of all loyal subjects, or faithful lovers of their country, were engaged on one side or other of the question; and Mark's Castle and Hillenfield Manor not only felt strongly, but luckily felt in unison. Mary of Orange had often been toasted between the Squire and the Knight; and, when it became certain that a bloodless revolution was effected, and the Protestant succession secured, bonfires blazed on the summit of Hillenfield Chase, more than rivalling those which lighted up the evening sky, over the hills bounding the domains of the De Bellyns.

By this time, the slight indisposition of Monica was converted into graver earnest. The dear one of her love was gone forth into exile with the king his master, and her heart almost broken with grief.

If anything could have cheered her, it would have been the perusal of a letter which Arthur Clifford, by a prodigality of bribery better suited to the measure of his love than of his fortune, contrived to get conveyed to her hands.

" Be not cast down, sweetest life !" wrote he ; " for, as sure as there is trust in God or faith in man, will I be true to the mistress of my soul. To me, my own Monica, I ask thee not to be faithful in return ; for, even were I prosperous and happy, faithful I know thou wouldst be.——How much more to a miserable exile, pursuing his duty to the throne and the altar, at all hazards, and with the certainty of a cruel absence from the only earthly thing he loves ! Even as I fear GOD and honour the king, my plighted wife, do I confide in THEE ! Thine, therefore, am I, even as thou art mine, in this world and in the next,

" A. C."

Such was the amulet which, in her hour of sickness, lay folded upon the heart of poor Monica ; affording patience under her sufferings, and a steady hope of better days to come.

Those better days, however, were slow of arrival. For the first time since the hour of her birth, ill feelings had sprung up between Monica and her parents; the old people pleading the cause of young De Bellyn with a degree of fervour arising from heartfelt interest in her welfare, but attributed by the unhappy girl to over-solicitude for the things of this world; and harsh words were often exchanged between those whose existence should have been as that of the stream in its channel, — compact, continuous, smooth,—flowing onwards in one harmonious course.

And thus poor Monica came to look with loathing upon the roof under which she was born. For, as no parents will believe, albeit most of them have experienced it in their turn, there is a moment in every life when filial love becomes subsidiary to that, to enforce which the Almighty Giver of the tables of the Law knew that no commandment was needful. Fain would Monica have cleaved to her plighted lover as to her lawful

husband; and those who spake of him de-
spitefully during his absence on an errand so
noble, ceased to be parents in her sight.

What tears she shed, poor girl!—what
sleepless nights she wore away!—What dreary
days, still longer than the nights in which she
was at least alone with her sorrows! In
summer, she loved to ramble in the calm, still
woods wherein had been their happy meetings;
though hard it seemed to find their verdure
still so refreshing, and the wild flowers car-
peting the paths so bright and fragrant, now
that no arm was entwined with hers to wander
among those green entanglements!—

Her heart ached again, even to breaking,
when, after the close of a seemingly interminable winter, she saw the tardy leaflets of
the oaks peep forth amid the lichens mossing
their branches, and the white lilies start up in
their green sheaths among the dead leaves of
the preceding autumn; and knew that a year
had come and gone since the departure of the
king, and the king's followers. And as yet,
no tidings of Arthur!

What need of tidings, however, to keep her affections changeless? — At the age of Monica, the fervour of the imagination suffices to keep alive the vestal lamp of Love. Wherever he might be, she was with him in the spirit; satisfied that his heart and soul were fixed upon herself.

Fortunately for Monica, Hugh de Bellyn was also absent from the country. Indignant at the haughty disdain with which he had been treated by the heiress, and faithfully devoted to the cause of William of Orange, on the king's proceeding to Ireland, he joined the army as a volunteer.

It might be (but this was a motive unavowed even to himself) that he hoped, while aiding to crush the rebellion of the Popish subjects of the Protestant king, to encounter the hated rival who had thwarted his happy prospects of alliance; but when his fancy conjured up, amidst his arduous duties of the camp, the peaked gables of the old mansion of the Hillenfields, embosomed in towering chestnut-trees after the fashion of old

Kentish mansions, little did he imagine how earnest were the prayers which rose from thence to Heaven for the discomfiture of the troops of which he formed a part!

The laughing face of Monica assumed a sternness almost worthy of a Judith,—nay, a degree of cruelty befitting the daughter of Herodias,—while she prayed to GOD that his bolts of vengeance might fall upon those who had driven their legitimate monarch into exile. — What needed it to add, who had parted her from her beloved Arthur!

But while this change was disfiguring the beauty of her youth, her fair, sweet countenance of better days was evermore smiling in the eyes of her betrothed! The chief object of Clifford in recommending that cunning court-enameller to the Hillenfields, had been the certainty of procuring, for a consideration, a copy of his work; and now, wherever he went, either as the gallant courtier of St. Germains or sturdy Captain of Derry, that portrait, concealed in his bosom, was as perpetual sunshine to his life.— The face was so lovely, so full of youth, and hope, and happiness!——Cold, hunger, and fatigue seemed easy to be borne, after cheering himself in the spring-like atmosphere of those eyes of love.

It needs not to fight over again that wretched campaign. Civil war is a thing too hideous to be lightly treated. Every one knows who conquered at the Boyne; no matter whether with right or might on his side. Suffice it that victory produced the offer of a peerage to Sir Gervase de Bellyn, and a dangerous wound to Captain Clifford—— the former, in requital of the services of his son,——the latter, of his own.

But of the wound and valour of poor Arthur, Monica heard not a syllable; whereas he gallant feats of young de Bellyn blazed in her eyes in the form of renewed bonfires and the acclamations of the country round, where, sooth to say, the grave young man was truly beloved. Not a mansion within twenty miles of Mark's Castle, in which thanksgivings were not offered for his safe return to his native country.

Still, the heart of Monica, the recluse, was
stedfast in its faith.   She heard nothing of
Arthur Clifford.   The family, by connexion
with which he had been naturalized in the
country, was, like himself, in exile.   She had
no means of inquiring whether he were alive
or dead; nay, it had become treason in well-
thinking circles so much as to advert to the
court of " the king over the water."   At the
end of the fourth year from the landing of
King William at Brixham, Monica knew no
more of the fate of Arthur Clifford than on
the day of his accompanying the Queen and
Prince of Wales in their precipitate flight.

Such was the state of affairs, when, one
day, by some unaccountable chance, a copy of
the *Mercure* newspaper, of European renown,
found its way to the sombre parlour of the
Manor.   How it came thither none could
guess, since birds of the air seldom constitute
themselves newspaper carriers.   Lord de
Bellyn (the second of that name, Gervase,
the first lord, being relieved from his gout
and other worldly troubles) was absent in

London on his parliamentary duties, and
must be absolved from all suspicion of con-
spiracy. But it was a singular coincidence
that this identical copy should contain an
account of a royal representation of one of
Racine's plays at St. Cyr before the court of
the exiled King of England, among whom
were expressly enumerated, " *Monsieur le
Capitaine Clifford et sa belle épouse.*"

A fortnight afterwards the Hillenfield
family repaired to town to prepare for the
union of the heiress. Yes !——Monica had
given her consent ; and that of her parents
and Lord de Bellyn had never been wanting.

It was a gorgeous wedding. The King
and Queen seemed to take pride and pleasure
in the occasion of doing honour to their
faithful servant. The nuptial ceremony was
performed in the royal chapel at Whitehall,
where William himself conferred the hand of
the daughter of the Hillenfields on the long-
expectant Lord of Mark's Castle.

After the ceremony, according to the
custom of the times, the happy couple re-

paired to their mansion, Bellyn House, in
Westminster, hard by Spring Gardens, to
keep state and festivity during the honey-
moon. It appeared to Monica that, at the
moment of stepping into her gilded coach,
some sort of disturbance arose among the
crowd. But this might be occasioned by the
petulance of one of the four spirited Flanders
mares, presented to her, with the equipage,
as a marriage-gift from the King.

For some following days, the attention of
the bride was too much taken up by the
courtly visits imposed upon her by her new
estate, to have leisure for noting the unusual
absence of her father. When she *did* inquire
of Mrs. Hillenfield, why he alone of all her
kinsfolk refrained from visiting Bellyn House,
she was informed that he was slightly indisposed, and that the physicians were apprehensive of contagion.

For why distress the feelings of the un-
suspecting bride by the afflicting disclosure
that this sudden indisposition arose from a
wound inflicted upon him by a travel-worn

Cavalier, who had attempted to force his way
in the Chapel-royal, at the moment her attention was excited by momentary disturbance? The wound was fortunately not
dangerous. A few weeks would suffice to
his recovery : and already, the frantic man,
by whom, in the exasperation of contention,
it had been given, was in durance, under
warrant of Chancery, not as a felon, but as a
lunatic.

For, alas! that stranger from foreign parts
was no other than Arthur Clifford ;—who, on
learning from some chance traveller from the
court of St. James's the approaching marriage of Monica, had, at all risks, and in
defiance of the decree of outlawry issued
against him, hurried to England, for the purpose of claiming, even at the foot of the
altar, his affianced bride ;—a bride whose
beauty and merit were every way qualified to
eclipse those of the *belle épouse* of his
brother Edward, the inopportune guest of
Louis XIV. at St. Cyr.

But recently arrived from a mission to

Rome, entrusted to him by the King, with the view to his perfect restoration from the effects of wounds received in his Irish campaign, the startling news of Monica's infidelity, received in all the exhaustion of an arduous and perilous expedition in the heat of the year, had such an influence on his mind, that, before he reached Whitehall, his perturbation of spirit amounted to insanity.

His first measure in London was to proceed to Bellyn House, in the hope of being in time to provoke his rival to a duel, and end by the sword the deadly enmity between them. But he was too late. The bridal train had already set off; and, long before he reached the chapel pointed out to him as the scene of solemnization, the nuptial anthem seemed to be sounding in his ears.——He was frantic——absolutely frantic.——The picture of Monica was still worn in his bosom, when, from afar, he beheld her assisted into her gorgeous carriage by the hated hand of Lord de Bellyn.

For *her* faithless heart, therefore, was probably destined the stroke which inflicted a flesh-wound on the shoulder of her father, who, unperceived by the tearful eyes of Monica, rushed in between her and her assailant. In the travel-stained man, some idler of the crowd having recognised the banished Arthur Clifford, the motive of the act was instantly supposed to be political. The partisan of King James was said to have attempted an assassination of the partisan of King William; and, during the outlawry of the heads of his family and the confiscation of their estates, it was considered an act of leniency on the part of the King that the offender was at once apprehended and sentenced to be confined for life as a lunatic, when it would have required no great stretch of the rigour of the law to condemn him to death as an assassin.

A Treasury mandate provided for the maintenance and security of the patient; and, as it was judged inadvisable to confine a man so nobly descended in a public hospital, he was consigned to a private lunatic asylum at Hammersmith, of which the celebrated Mead was visiting physician, and where his companions in misfortune belonged to his own condition of life.

When first incarcerated, the malady of poor Arthur, stimulated by fever, was of the most furious and alarming kind. But the inflammation of the brain having been overcome, he relapsed into a gentle melancholy—a species of childish despair—which his medical attendants soon pronounced to be incurable. For hours and hours together, would he sit conversing with his beloved medallion,—the portrait of Monica;—of which, throughout his misfortunes, he had never been deprived. It was his treasure—his companion—his friend—his love—his wife: and often was he heard conjuring that fair face to smile upon him, and those lips to answer to his passionate appeals—as though the portrait were endowed with instinct and volition.

> Anon, as gentle as the female dove,
> Ere yet her golden couplets are disclosed,
> His silence would sit drooping.

Over such a state of mind, the lapse of years passeth as that of a day. All seasons and their change were alike to Arthur. Sleep, exercise, meals, inflicted upon him as in punishment, at the word of command, or sound of a bell, rendered days, months, and years, as one continuous void. Spring, summer, autumn, winter, brought no change to his benumbed faculties. All he saw beneath the sky was that one loved face.

Thus absorbed, even the gradual whitening of his hair, even the subsiding of his complexion to a faded yellow, even the wrinkles gradually plaiting his wasted cheeks, were undreamed of by the poor maniac: and, though William of Orange and his rival of the House of Stuart had sunk together into the grave,——though the victories of Anne had filled the ears of Europe with wonder, and her heirless reign had been followed by the accession of the House of Hanover,——not a single new perception had reached the mind of Clifford since the day on which he beheld his Monica led from the altar by her bridegroom.

Yet since then, the cedar-tree in the high-walled garden of his miserable asylum had doubled its height. Since then, the noble-looking youth of five-and-twenty had dwindled into the decrepit man of sixty-five. Still young with perpetual childishness of spirit, — still young with unchanging fervency of love, — for *him* the court of St. Germains retained its pride, and Monica her beauty !—

Is such a state of mind to be pitied?—Is a life passed in this puerile innocence, of joy, really deplorable?—It is for hereafter to decide.—But, even in *this* world, the fond idolator of Lady de Bellyn was fated to a strange revolution of feeling.

It happened that, at the close of the disastrous Rising in the North, in the year 1715, a young Northumbrian, of the name of Beaumont, who had shared the misfortunes of Derwentwater and narrowly escaped his fate, was, by the mercy of Government, placed in the asylum so long assigned to Arthur Clifford. Between the two, a sort of sympathy arose. The attention of the latter being excited towards the stranger by pious and loyal mention of the name of Stuart, to young Beaumont he fondly exhibited the Madonna of his devotions; to young Beaumont, he boasted of the beauty and fidelity of the Monica who was waiting his escape from durance to reward him with the rich treasure of her hand.

The new-comer, on the other hand, confided in mysterious secrecy to his gray-headed friend, that he was the Chevalier Bayard, consecrated by the patriarch of Constantinople to head the armies of Jame III., King of Great Britain, Ireland, and Nova Zembla, and maliciously imprisoned by the Elector of Hanover, in order to prevent his taking the field. To escape and make his way to the camp of his lawful sovereign was the absorbing idea of the poor maniac; and, having prevailed upon his new friend to share his enterprise, so ardent was his desire for liberty, and so cunning the combination of his plans, that, one fine morning in May, ere the bell of the asylum rang for breakfast, the unfortunate pair dropped from that lofty garden-wall into the fields below, and before the alarm was raised, had reached the suburb of Pimlico.

Here, a diversity of opinion arose between them ; the Chevalier Bayard was for getting into a stage coach, and proceeding at once to Berwick-upon-Tweed, to raise the standard of revolt ; while the sad-faced, tremulous old man, his companion, insisted that they should first proceed to Bellyn House, in Spring Gardens, that he might be armed by the fair hands of Monica for the fight. Restoration to the stir and tumult of the common earth, from which he had been nearly half a century divided, had so far restored him to his senses, as to remind him of the fatal events of his last day of worldly freedom, and that the object of his passion was now the wife of another.

Hurrying along the Birdcage Walk, therefore, they pursued their way across St. James's Park to the extremity of the Mall ;

and, by dint of inquiries, which appeared to be those of gentlemen strange to the town, succeeded in reaching the mansion of Lord De Bellyn without exciting inordinate curiosity.

The old man was growing every moment more incoherent, when Beaumont (who, on every point but politics, was perfectly self-possessed,) summoned the servants of the house in the usual manner, and desired admittance to their lady.

" What names," the servants inquired, " should they have the honour to announce ?" And, to the ears of the lacqueys, those of " Captain Clifford and the Chevalier Bayard" presented nothing extraordinary.

Having followed the servants up the grand staircase, and across two or three dreary, stately chambers, they were ushered into a small withdrawing room, the entrance to which was sheltered by a folding screen of Japan.

" Not here—not *her !*" — cried Clifford, seizing the arm of one of the servants, as he

was placing chairs opposite to a tall, skinny
figure, attired in one of the black mantles
then in vogue, and having the hair drawn up
and powdered over her pinched forehead.

" I told you I had business of importance
with Lady de Bellyn......"

" *I* am Lady de Bellyn, sir!" said the
cracked treble of the dowager, as she placed
her snuffbox on the table, and motioned the
strangers to seats.

" Ha! ha! ha! ha! *You* Lady de Bellyn?"
exclaimed both visitors at once——the servants
having, on an incautious signal from their
lady, already withdrawn —— " *You*——witch——
hag——Hecate——howlet in a bush!"——added
Clifford with frantic indignation, " *you*, my
own lovely Monica!——"

And the two maniacs began to jibber, and
point with their lean fingers at the terrified
woman, who, after a life of care, had found
comfort in the practices of an austere devotion.

Already she had risen, and was darting at
the bell, when Clifford forestalled the move-

ment by seizing her hand. "Look at these withered claws!" cried he, pointing out their articulations to his companion; "and see what this beldam would persuade me to be the hands on which my lips have hung so oft,—— the white, white hands of my Monica!——"

At the sound of a name so long unpronounced in her ears, the whole truth rushed into the mind of the terrified dowager. Aware of Clifford's aberration of intellect and long confinement, she only too truly conjectured that the lunatic of decrepit form and lacklustre eye before her was no other than the impassioned lover of her youth.——What was to become of her?——He had doubtless escaped from confinement in order to inflict some long concocted project of revenge!——But woman's wit, even on the verge of threescore years and ten, is fertile in expedients.

"I am indeed your own Monica," said she; "though so ruined in health by the machinations of the Hanoverian government, as to be nearly unrecognizable. When the King shall enjoy his own again, I too am to be restored to the comeliness of youth. But his Majesty is now in the house. Suffer me to apprize him that his faithful servant is come to do him homage in his misfortunes.——Let me summon the Duke of Perth.——Let me ring for the Lord Chamberlain.——"

And in her agony of fear lest the imposture should be too gross for the impaired perceptions of her guests, and every moment expecting one or other of them to spring at her throat and strangle her on the spot, her voice faltered as she spoke, and her parchment cheek was visited, for the first time for twenty years, by a hectic flush.

To her unspeakable joy, however, two grotesque bows conveyed their consent; and, having pulled the bell-ribbon till it broke, the servants burst into the room. "Seize those madmen, and send for a troop from the Horse Guards to secure them!" cried the poor old lady as she sank swooning into her chair.

The maniacs were accordingly reconveyed to their place of confinement. And now, for the first time, durance became insupportable to the unfortunate Clifford. The spell of his consolation was broken; the blossoms of his perpetual spring had faded; the sunshine of his eternal summer disappeared; his dream—his dream of love and joy —the dream which had brightened half a century of cheerless existence—was vanished for ever.

The sight of his beloved picturehad become hateful to him. Sometimes, a glimpse of it would melt him to tears; but far oftener provoke him into blasphemies fearful to think of. The struggle was not of long continuance. In the course of the following winter, he expired, pronouncing, in his last moments, with clasped hands and streaming eyes, the fondly-remembered name of—Monica.[1]

[1] A similar incident, related of a noble family in France, has been recounted in various memoirs of the time, and given rise to a popular drama.

A VISION OF A ROYAL BALL.

It is the strangest thing in the world
(wrote the young Viscountess Trevor in her
favourite commonplace-book, the blank end of
which had been, since her residence at Trevor
Court, converted into a journal)—it is the
strangest thing in the world that Lord and
Lady Castlemoat should see so much to oppose
in our taste for living in the country. If Arthur
were in Parliament, or if we had a house in
town of our own, the case would be different.
But since, when in London, we have to choose
between a visit to *them*, or a residence in an
hotel, (as costly as it is comfortless,) what
more natural than that we should prefer remaining at Trevor Court; a place they have
given up to us, and which, during the last year,
we have converted into a paradise on earth?

Still, though we are dreadfully in the way whenever we have occasion to spend a day or two in Grosvenor Square, and though Lady Sophia and Lady Adelaide contrive to make me feel it before I have been an hour in the house, scarcely a day passes without a letter from my mother-in-law, complaining of our obstinacy in remaining in the country, now there are neither field-sports nor neighbours to help us through our time. Lady Castlemoat seems to think that by *my* influence, Trevor has been persuaded to mope himself to death, merely because his *parvenue* wife has not courage to confront the scrutiny of the *beau monde* !

How little do my mother and sisters-in-law understand me; and how small is my chance of changing their opinion! It would be like talking to a blind man of the rainbow, to assure them of the delight we take in our improvements here, and the advantage their progress has derived from our being on the spot. The only answer I ever obtain from the girls is, that " when in former days they visited

Trevor Court, it looked wonderfully like a state prison, and that they should be sorry ever to see it again ;" while their mother has more than once given me to understand that Arthur is spoiling the place.

" It is not to be expected, my dear Lady Trevor," said she," that your father's villa in Hertfordshire should have inspired you with a taste for antiquities.   Still, I was in hopes that my son had too much respect for all that is venerable in our family-place, to vulgarize it by modern improvements."

I assured her, and with truth, that nothing had been done to alter the antique aspect of the old mansion; that every fragment of painted glass has been carefully replaced, and that my flower-garden is placed at a sufficient distance from the house to produce no change in the approach.   But I cannot persuade her to believe that the filling up of the moat was a necessary precaution; or that the typhus-fever, the perpetual recurrence of which in the household rendered a residence here impracticable, had never reappeared since the destruction of those stagnant waters. All the answer I obtain is, that " when people are not accustomed to that sort of feudal habitation, they think it dull ;" and that " those who are *bored* often fancy themselves *ill*."

Useless to assure her that I have never known a day's ill health, or a moment's *ennui* at Trevor Court, or that the mortality which prevailed there while it remained the family residence, was long before I was born. I am now so accustomed to find every thing I say or do converted by the Trevor family into indications of my plebeian origin, that I have ceased to vindicate my tastes and opinions. Argument might some day or other lead to contention ; and so long as I am assured of Arthur's approval and affection, better they should think me stupid than petulant or self-assured. Let my husband only be content to remain quietly with me at Trevor Court, enjoying our rides and drives this delicious spring weather ; leaving *them* to their noisy round of hollow dissipations.

But I am beginning to be half afraid !——

Lord Castlemoat's last letter accused him of inertness,—of want of energy—of indifference to the state of the country, in a tone of such severe reprobation, that Arthur is beginning to look about him, as if afraid of having mislaid the ambition which the people are apt to dignify by the name of patriotism.

Last year he seemed almost *glad* to have lost his election.   But within these last few days, he has become terribly interested in the debates ; and the other evening observed that, " After all, it was a bad thing for a man who had so large a stake in the country, and a part to play hereafter in its history, to get out of parliamentary habits."

I ventured to observe that my father always asserted the lower House to be a bad school for the Upper.   To which he answered in a manner more abrupt than I ever heard him use before, " What should your father know about it, who had not set foot in the House of Lords half-a-dozen times in his life !—"

Alas ! what would become of me, were the contemptuous feelings which the rest of the

family are at so little pains to conceal concerning the mercantile origin of my fortune, to
extend to my husband ! From Arthur, I could
never forgive what from *them* I accept with a
smile.   That which, with his sisters, amounts
to an absurdity, would be in him the basest
ingratitude. ˙ And were I once conscious—
once calmly and reasonably conscious of being
insulted by my husband in the same cold-
blooded manner I have been by Lady Castlemoat and her daughters, there would be an end
to my happiness—and *his !*

For it is no longer in their power to disguise from me, or in mine to disguise from
myself, that, *but* for this fortune of mine, of
which they now affect to speak so scornfully,
Arthur could not have married at all.   A few
hundreds a year are all Lord Castlemoat is
able to spare his son; and how could a man
of Arthur's liberal habits have subsisted on
that ?—Though vain enough to believe—nay,
happy enough to be certain—that, had I been
penniless, he would have entertained the same
affection for me, and felt the same desire to

make me his wife, the marriage would have been impossible!——Thankful therefore ought I to be to Providence for those ample means with which I am sometimes, in a moment of petulance, tempted to quarrel, as affording a pretext for the bitter impertinence of the Trevors.

Let them, however, be as contemptuous as they please, they cannot efface from my memory the period when " the heiress" was an object of as warm a courtship to *them* as to dear Arthur!——How they used to besiege me with invitations,——and how completely my poor father saw through it all!——Had he not discerned the manly straightforwardness of Arthur as plainly as the base motives of the family, never would he have allowed me to enter their house. Still less would he have determined on that noble provision for me in the event of my becoming Trevor's wife, which, alas! his sudden death afforded me the power of making my own act and deed. Had he lived, these people would never have ventured to exhibit the feelings which were doubtless from first to last rankling in their hearts.

From all this, I must exempt my father-in-law. The cold politeness of Lord Castlemoat, which at first I thought so repellent, has never failed me.——*His* conduct has never varied.——He always treated me with ceremonious deference, and does so still; and but for his exhortations and remonstrances to his son, I should fancy he viewed our conduct with the same formal approval he expressed at the first meeting between him and my poor father, to decide upon the question of settlements.

But if I run on in this way I shall become as bitter as my sisters-in-law!——One ought not to be *too* frank, I am afraid, even with oneself; and by indulging in angry feelings towards my husband's family, and cherishing them in secret, this tranquil, peaceful place would forfeit half its charm. Better exert myself to subdue the enemy at once!——I have half a mind to throw my journal into the fire.

May 2nd.——What a charming ride !——I was afraid it might have turned out ill ; for I had quite forgotten the proposition made me last night, by my husband, to accompany him to see the orchards at Hagglestone,——which are in full blossom and perfect beauty ; and when the mare was brought to the door, had not begun to dress for my ride.

Arthur cannot bear being kept waiting !—— Luckily, he had the morning papers to look over, and did not seem to think me long in putting on my habit.

As to being cross when we were fairly on horseback and sauntering under those glorious avenues, so beautiful just now with the first fresh tender verdure of spring, it was out of the question. Even Lady Sophia and her sister, had they been of our party, must have been good-humoured, for once in their lives. The birds were singing so gaily, and the Hagglestone orchards so white with their bridal blossoms, that every thing had the appearance of a *fête*. In the lane near Mapletoft, we met our worthy curate ; who tells

me the school will certainly be opened at the
end of the month.——Thirty-six poor children
already on my list !——

The only drawback on the pleasure of my
ride arose from Arthur's frequent recurrence
to the confirmation contained in the morning
papers of the report of a Masque at the
palace. The epoch is fixed, it seems, for the
reign of George II., and the ball is to take
place in a month. Thank goodness ! It will
serve to occupy the attention of Lady Castlemoat and my sisters-in-law, and make them
forget Trevor Court and its offences.——I am
vexed, however, to see how deep an interest
Arthur takes in the event. How little do I
care *now* for any thing that is going on in
London !——

4*th*.——A letter from Lady Castlemoat !——
an unusual honour,——for I had not heard
from her these two months. Her letter is
full of nothing but the ball. Though the
invitations are not yet issued, she has already
decided on her own , and her daughters'
dresses, and her chief object in writing to me

appears to be to engage, for Sophia, the use of my pearls. Of course she might be certain of having them. What use have I for such things in the country at this time of year? " Being afraid I might be applied to by my friend, Lady Mary Herbert, she chose to secure them in time."

My mother-in-law does not know Lady Mary!—Even at a royal ball, and on so peculiar an occasion, nothing would persuade *her* to appear in borrowed plumes. Mary Herbert is truth itself. Never was there a person so punctiliously and rigidly honest. Absent or present, I have confidence in *her* as in my own soul. Nothing that any human being could say or do would persuade me Lady Mary had spoken slightingly of me behind my back; or been guilty of unkindness or unfairness to any living thing.

Since the arrival of his mother's letter, Arthur has talked more than ever of the ball. He even hints that had I accepted his mother's proposal to go to town for the last drawing-room, I should certainly have been invited.

But we could scarcely have appeared in London for that single *fête,* and I am well reconciled to know no more of it than is to be learned from the newspapers.

When the first Masque was given, before I was out, I remember every one getting tired to death of hearing it talked about. The false excitement and interest it created was said to spoil the rest of the London season. If this second *fête* should spoil the *country* season, *quel malheur !*——

5th.——Yesterday, after dinner, Arthur went fast asleep, which was not wonderful, as we had taken a long walk together across the park in the afternoon; and the weather is now growing almost too summerish for walking in the middle of the day. I was so unlucky as to wake him by drawing down the blinds to prevent the setting sun from shining full into his eyes; and then, as men are apt to do, he began to protest he had never been asleep.

I am afraid I did not manage to look convinced I had been mistaken; for, as if to

punish me, he instantly began again about
the ball ; telling me (which I had certainly
heard often enough before,) that at the last
Masque he appeared in the armour worn by
one of his ancestors at the battle of Crécy ;
while his partner, that beautiful Lady Ida de
Tracy, wore a hawking dress copied from one
of her ancestresses of the same date.

I suppose my foolish susceptibility is in
fault. But I am beginning to hate the sound
of the words " ancestor" or " ancestress"
pronounced by one of the Trevors ! I always
fancy they accompany it with a look that
renders it personal. Had my poor father lived,
such fancies would have never entered my
head. He was so much beloved,—so much
respected, both in public and private life, that
no one presumed to convey disparagement to
him. Now he is gone, I, who have so little
to recommend or sustain me in the world,
can hardly hope to escape without a few of
the rubs which great people are fond of in-
flicting upon little—even when the little have
been courted for purposes of their own.

But I am making myself *less* than little, by ascribing so much importance to the petty vexations of life!——Happy as I am in my lot, surely I can afford to allow the Trevors the gratuitous triumph of feeling themselves my superiors ?——

6th.——To-day, Arthur was smitten with a fancy for visiting the picture-gallery, which old Mrs. Casterton keeps as carefully locked as though she thought the family honour safer in *her* keeping than ours. Since the first month I came here, after my marriage, I have literally only once entered it. One of the conditions made by my father-in-law on ceding Trevor Court to us was, that whatever alterations we might make in the place, the old pleasaunce and state apartments of the west wing should remain untouched ; and this, I think, our own good taste would have determined, even had it not been enforced by Lord Castlemoat.

As these are the only portions of the place exhibited to strangers, and consequently a considerable source of profit to the house-

keeper, old Mrs. Casterton, to whom the prohibition of the earl was, I suppose, a secret,
did not behold without fear and trembling
the arrival of so many designers, bricklayers,
masons, and gardeners.   The old lady evidently thought her dominions in danger;
and once or twice, when I sent my maid,
Wilson, to ask for the keys of the state
apartments to indulge my curiosity by a more
deliberate view of the pictures than Arthur
had allowed me when we visited them together, she chose to bring them to me in
person, with a solemn harangue about the
sacredness of the trust; insisting that I
should summon her again to receive them
from my hands, when my visit to the west
wing was over.   Even the old housekeeper
could not fancy me *at home* in the spot containing the grand family portraits of the
Trevors !——

I was so annoyed by this, happening as it
did in presence of Wilson, and giving rise to
her pert comments on " the haughtiness of
even the servants of the old family towards

her poor dear young lady," that I could give only a divided attention to the pictures; and when Arthur sent to Mrs. Casterton this morning for the keys, was as much pleased at the idea of visiting them, as if I had never seen them before.

Yet how well I remember the imposing ffect produced upon my mind by my first introduction into those vast, echoing rooms, with their bright, dry-rubbed floors, with a strip of scarlet cloth running along each,—and their close, stagnant atmosphere. The old pictures in their tarnished frames—many of them bearing the arms and coronet of the Trevors,—grim knights in armour, or judges in ermine, looking solemn and earnest about nothing, and scarcely more lively on canvas, than in their marble effigies, kneeling under their mildewed escutcheons in the chancel of the parish church!—The furniture of these state rooms, consisting of old cabinets and marble tables, with stately velvet fauteuils, either white or gilded, apparently made for giants to sit on,—the old state bed, with its

dingy ostrich plumes, said to have been slept
in by Queen Elizabeth,—the gloomy banqueting hall, — the painted chapel — though as
little tempting as can be conceived in the
way of habitation, inspired me with some
deference towards the dignities of the family
I had so recently entered; more especially
when Mrs. Casterton, in her high-crowned
cap and plaited apron, curtseyed respectfully
while explaining the origin and history of the
ancestral pictures.   She had not then learned
the mystery of my city connexions; and
could not conceive it *possible* that the heir of
all the Trevors should have married any thing
below the daughter of a duke.

When we entered the rooms this morning,
the air seemed closer than ever; and when
Arthur complained of it to the old lady, who,
in spite of his express orders, hobbled up to
escort us, she replied that " the state apartments were seldom or ever opened now;" that
" folks having heard how things were turned
topsy-turvy at Trevor Court, concluded *nothing* had been respected, and felt no further

curiosity to visit the spot;" an impertinence for which my husband rebuked her so sharply, and dismissed her from further attendance upon us so abruptly, that I doubt whether my subsequent visit to the housekeeper's room, or the present I made the old lady, on restoring the keys, sufficed to pacify her resentment.

As soon as she was gone, Arthur took upon himself the task of explaining the pictures, and we began to enjoy ourselves. Some of them are very fine;—all, very interesting. Holbein, Zucchero, Rubens, Van Dyk, Old Franck, Lely, Kneller, Reynolds, have done their best to perpetuate the memory of persons otherwise born to be forgotten. For I cannot remember in the records of the field or the cabinet of our national history, mention of one of the names I saw inscribed on those tarnished frames.

" All fine fellows, no doubt, in their time !" said Arthur, as he laughingly introduced me to his ancestors. " But the best thing about them, I fancy, was what they were forced to

G 2

leave behind, namely, their broad lands in
Yorkshire, and their stately castle in Kent;
to say nothing of this dear tumbledown old
place, which makes us both so happy!"

And he proceeded to point out to me the
bearded effigy of Sir Harstonge de Trevor, in
his trunk hose; on whose monument, bearing the date of 1580, is the quaint epitaph
of,

> That I spent, that I had,
> That I gave, that I have,
> That I left, that I lost.

Not " lost" to *us*, however, for he was the
chief founder of Trevor Court.

In a vestibule adjoining the picture-gallery
are a few portraits belonging to the last century; several of them faded things, in crayons,
that look like mere ghosts of pictures.   Besides these, are several by Kneller and Gervas,
and two by Angelica Kauffmann, painted
when Sir Joshua was her suitor.

" My mother's letter desired me to look
over these relics," said he.   " Our best
pictures are in Grosvenor Square or at Castle-

moat ; but there are no portraits among them.
And she is anxious, it seems, to appear at the
Powder Ball in something especially Tre-
voresque."

I offered my aid and advice : but, alas ! we
found nothing relating to the epoch in question, except a stern old countess in a widow's
costume of the time of Queen Anne, with
the towering lawn coif and black crape veil,
which the said dowager Lady Trevor wore
till the day of her death in the reign of
George II. ; and the portrait of her daughter,
Lady Barbara—a beautiful girl of eighteen—
maid of honour to Queen Caroline, when
Princess of Wales.

" Whom did she marry ?" I inquired, involuntarily interested by the piquant archness
of her countenance, and extreme elegance of
her dress.

" My great grand uncle, who took her
name. Lady Barbara was the heiress of the
Trevors," said Arthur, throwing open the
windows of the vestibule, and as much re-
freshed as myself by the burst of warm spring

air, scented by a thousand flowers, and above all, by the fresh young herbage of a thousand pastures. "Not much better than she should be, I am afraid!—But heiresses are seldom good for much. I shall write my mother word I could find nothing likely to do her credit; so she must put up with being a fifteenth Maria Leczinska, or something of that kind. By Jove! yonder is John, bringing round the horses. Don't you think the mare goes a little lame?—No, she was treading on a stone. Come, get on your habit, like a good girl, while I send back the keys to old Mother Casterton. I never set foot in the uninhabited rooms of the west wing, without getting the headach or the vapours."

Vapours *or* headach, a good gallop across the hills sufficed for his cure; and it was a mere pretence of being still indisposed which caused him to delegate to *me* the task of answering Lady Castlemoat's letter, and assuring her there was nothing among the family pictures likely to furnish her with a becoming costume.

I have obeyed his injunctions; but to-morrow I will look through a French work I have noticed in the library, containing portraits of the beauties of the court of Louis XV., which may perhaps supply us with something more to the purpose.

7th.——Last night, I was sitting at my work-table, putting the finishing stitches to the Greek smoking-cap I have been embroidering for Arthur; and as he usually reads to me from tea till bed-time, and had got the last volume of " Lord Malmesbury's Correspondence " open before him, I naturally concluded he was about to begin. But after a dead silence of ten minutes, during which his eyes were fixed upon the book, he suddenly burst forth with, " I wonder whether it would have been contrary to etiquette for me to wear the Red Riband ?"——

For a moment, I fancied he had fallen asleep, and was dreaming; but no !——on glancing at his face, I saw he was not only wide awake, but unusually full of animation; *so* wide awake, indeed, that I was forced to ask an explanation of his strange apostrophe.

"Of what Red Riband are you talking, dear Trevor?" said I.

"Of Sir Harry Chamberlain's. If I had been invited to the Queen's ball, you should have gone as Lady Barbara Trevor, and I as her gallant spouse."

"The ex-maid of honour in the pink and green sacque?" said I.

"Exactly!—The young colonel in the Guards, who afterwards figured as her liege lord, became in due time a Knight of the Bath. You would have looked charmingly, Minnie, in that fantastic dress, with the little chaplet of roses, and the diamond aigrette sparkling over one ear. Powder would certainly have become you.—Powder becomes all women with good eyes and dark eyebrows.—I should like beyond everything to see you in powder."

"I will not return the compliment by saying I should like to see you in a queue and side-curls. I prefer you in your shooting-jacket," said I.

" Shooting-jackets begin to be rather out of place at this season of the year," retorted Arthur; " particularly this cursed late spring, when I *do* believe the May-fly will not make its appearance on the water till Midsummer! When shooting and hunting are over, and fishing not begun, what the deuce is a man to do with himself in the country?"

It was not for me to answer " ride, or walk, or drive with his wife, as you are doing every day." But glad enough I was, when, discouraged by my awkward silence, he betook himself in earnest to " Lord Malmesbury's Letters," as a substitute for conversation.

10*th*.—Is *ennui* an infectious disorder?—For the last few days, I have felt almost as much hypped as my husband. I wander about the place like a ghost; and have not found courage even to write a word in my journal. When our good curate came from Mapletoft to arrange with me yesterday morning about the opening of the school, I was seized with such a fit of cold shivers at the mere idea of

the exertion, that he could not help inquiring
whether I was ill.   I answered in the affirmative, as the shortest way of closing his visit.
I *could* not tell *him* that I was only *bored.*
BORED !——I remember the time when that
word used to give me a dislike to the speaker !
I have often vowed it should never pass my
lips !——Heigho !

15*th*.——What a fortunate——and yet, what
an *un*fortunate occurrence !   After all, we
are actually invited to the ball.   Cards were
sent by the Lord Chamberlain to Grosvenor
Square, for Trevor and myself, as well as for
the rest of the family.   Arthur will be enabled
to wear Sir Harry Chamberlain's "Red Riband"
after all, and Lady Castlemoat has already decided, *for me,* upon the pink and green sacque !

Rather hard that I am to be allowed no
choice in such a trifle.   My husband is perhaps right that the colours will be becoming,
and that it is better to appear in the dress of
some member of the Trevor family prominent
at the period in request.   But still...Well ! no
matter !——

16*th*.——I never saw a person more childishly elated than Arthur at the prospect of this unexpected pleasure ; but his family, as if resolved to curtail me of my share, have already dropped a few bitters into the cup. Lady Castlemoat writes again to inquire whether it is my wish to appear in her minuet, and if so, to consider seriously, before she assigns a place to me, " whether I have sufficient *à plomb* for so public an exhibition ?"

" Unused as you are to such scenes," she observes, " and unpractised in the courtly dance of the minuet, you must come to town and take lessons without loss of time, if you intend to make your appearance in my set."

Of whom or what this " set " may consist, I know not. My sisters-in-law, of course—— and Lady Mary Herbert, probably—for the Castlemoats are decidedly making up to her for Frederick. At all events, having no wish to disgrace them, I have written, as courteously as I can, to say that most likely I shall not dance at all.   For this I have given no reason—my motive being one which at present I do not wish to assign.

All the morning, I have been busy making a water-colour sketch from the oil-portrait of Lady Barbara Trevor, to send up to town to Madame Louise, who is to make my dress, as well as those of my sisters-in-law.   At first, I made the attempt in the vestibule of the west wing.   But Arthur, who found me shivering there, insisted that the picture should be taken down for my convenience, and removed into my dressing-room; and when old Mrs. Casterton remonstrated, and talked about being "responsible to my lord, his father, for the family pictures," he answered her in a tone I never heard him use before, especially to a woman; and bade her remember that so long as *he* resided at Trevor Court, she was responsible to *him !*——

I expected the old lady would break out into further impertinence.   But she seemed struck dumb with amazement, and hobbled out of the room as mute and meek as a mouse.

Arthur was charmed——too much charmed with my sketch. Unaccustomed to notice such things, he fancies me quite an artist; and was even foolish enough to write and beg his mother would show the drawing to Chalon before she threw it away upon a mantuamaker.

Usually, such tasks delight me. But I grew sick to death of the pink and green sacque before I had half made out its quillings and plaitings. And yet how strangely one becomes interested in copying any human face not purely ideal!——The endeavour to catch the expression of the eye, and seize the physiognomy of the features, induces one to search into the indications of character contained in every muscle. Though till yesterday I never wasted a thought upon Barbara Lady Trevor, I have now cogitated upon her and her history, till I begin to regret Arthur's quarrel with Mrs. Casterton; but for which I should certainly apply to the old lady for an explanation of my hus-

band's " not much better than she should
be."

I wonder what she was, besides a beauty
and an heiress?——Wit, or, at all events, repar-
tee, lurks in the arch corners of her pretty
mouth. But the eyes convey an expression
of which I stood almost in awe while trans-
ferring it to my copy. Lady Castlemoat
would have found no occasion, with *such* a
daughter-in-law, to complain of want of
usage du monde or self-possession; but then
she sprang from a race whose nobility was
ancient in the days of William the Conqueror.
She had some pretence for self-possession.
Heigho!——I wonder what makes me trouble
myself so foolishly concerning her or her
adventures?—— I seem to think of nothing
else!

19*th*.——How provoking!——Lady Castlemoat
writes to compliment me on my discretion in
not attempting the minuet, and to inquire
whom I wish to appoint my *costumière*,——
Louise being so busy that she will not hear of
undertaking my dress.

Satisfied that my mother-in-law would put no small share of ill-will into the execution of my commission, I have determined to have the pink and green sacque made up at home. Wilson is a capital work-woman; and as we have the precise model before us, there can be no difficulty. I shall thus escape the annoyance of going to town ten days before the time; and I am beginning to feel much too unwell for any extra exertion.

24th.—How sick I am, already, of the whole thing! Arthur has been to town about his dress, and returned yesterday raving of bags, and swords, and red-heeled shoes. He saw the minuet practised at his mother's; who pretends now to be affronted at our having declined to belong to it—though she certainly did little enough to persuade us. Lady Mary Herbert, he says, dances it divinely, and his sisters have been taking lessons of Lucile Grahn. Every body,— even grave men of forty, and women of any age,—are learning to dance!

All this I have luckily escaped. But not so Wilson's stupidity. My stomacher is three times too wide; and though she declares that it cannot be an inch smaller to exhibit all my jewels (which Arthur insists upon my wearing), it is far beyond the admeasurement of my little person. I am tired of fighting it over with the poor woman; and still more so, of pointing out to her, one by one, the details of that horrible picture, which I have been forced to study and study till it seems to have grown a part of myself!

I shall be glad when I get it out of my dressing-room; for the wicked eyes appear to follow me wherever I go, and the arch smile to mock me for my assiduity in rendering myself a mere copy of its fantastic graces!—I suppose it is because I am ill. But both the face and figure have taken possession of me. When I tried on my dress last night, I could not help turning round, with a shudder, to see whether the picture, *my original*, had deserted its frame.—I was even silly enough to desire Wilson to turn the face to the wall.

It seemed to be making game of us.——I could almost fancy I heard a faint laugh !——

All this must proceed from indisposition. What would Arthur think of me were he aware that I had imagined or recorded such nonsense !

*　　　*　　　*　　　*

What a horrible scene !——How frightful,—— how bewildering !——Vainly do I press my hands to my head and heart to shut out the cruel impression. All still lives and breathes around me, as though for the remainder of my days I were to be haunted by the influence of that fatal ball !

But let me endeavour to retrace calmly the details of my sufferings.

When at length, full dressed and faint from the exertion, I entered the yellow drawing-room at Buckingham House, surrounded by all that is brilliant or beautiful of the noble throng usually assembled in the stately spot, much as I had previously heard of the marvels awaiting me, I was overpowered and en-chanted by the completeness of the illusion.

The whole court, and even the attendants and musicians, were arrayed with the utmost minuteness of precision in the garb of an epoch, the costume of which I always considered frightful, till I beheld it displayed on persons so attractive as those of Lady Jocelyn, Lady Ormonde, Mrs. Hope, and numberless others, to whose strangely-altered faces I could scarcely assign a name.

Nothing will persuade me, however, that the period thus simulated ever really exhibited so gorgeous a show of luxury as the representation of it on which I gazed. During the lapse of the last century, Golconda has been hourly yielding up her treasures, and the fishers of Ormus and mines of the Cordilleras producing new gems of wondrous growth; and how brightly did they shine, amid the enhancing whiteness of those powdered locks, or the folds of those rich brocades, or cloths of gold and silver, too heavy to rustle as one passed!

After the first glance of admiration elicited by the magic influence of the scene, however,

it was neither those fair faces nor the perfect
success of the attempt to endow them with
new graces, that occupied my attention. To
my shame be it spoken, I thought only of myself! Harassed by the apprehension evinced
throughout the preparations for the ball by
my mother-in-law and her daughters, lest I
should not do them honour on an occasion so
public, I could not divert my attention from
the graceful draperies of my pink and green
sacque, or the lustre of my costly stomacher.
For the first time in my life, all I sought in
those resplendent rooms was a mirror in
which I might survey my own person.

It was not till I reached the gallery that
my vanity was fully gratified. Having made
my way thither, on Arthur's arm, on pretence
of wishing to see the queen emerge from the
dancing room after the first minuet, unspeakable was my triumph when I saw advance to
meet me a figure which was that of the
heiress of the House of Trevor stepped from
her frame; and perceived that the quivering
light of a certain jewelled stomacher and

aigrette, and the glistening richness of the
lustring, enhanced by quillings of old point,
were mere reflections in the opposite glass !——
Though tired and eager for a seat, I had not
courage to forsake the beauteous figure I was
surveying, by placing myself on the bench
below the glass. I would hear of nothing
but a turn in the gallery, where, on pretence
of admiring the showy belles and beaux ranged
in rows along the wall, many a scarcely
furtive glance did I cast towards the mirrors
reproducing the scene. I was dying to judge
the effect of the rouge and patches which,
for the first time, adorned my face. The
spirit of Lady Barbara's coquetry seemed to
have taken possession of me.——But of all
earthly intoxications, what so bewildering as
the intoxication of vanity? Weeks given to
the preparation of my dress,——days to the
study of the most becoming movements
assorted with it, —— and hours to attiring
myself in its complicated draperies, —— had
so excited my spirits, that on witnessing
the triumphant success of my labours, I

lost sight of every other object in the world !——

In no other manner can I account for my strange inconsistency in accepting with glee the proposition of Lady Sophia Trevor, that I should fill in her mother's minuet the place of Lady Clanstephen, who, not yet arrived, was supposed to be detained by the unpunctuality of Louise. Conscious that I had not forgotten my school-day lessons with Madame Michau, I was enchanted by the prospect of becoming the mark of general observation. The original owner of the pink and green sacque could not have been more contemptibly elated !——

I saw that Trevor did not wish me to dance. Yet I persisted,——persisted though my partner was to be Mary Herbert's brother,——the only one of the former pretendants to my hand. against whose future acquaintance Arthur ever took exception.

"Lord Herbert is the only one of them who really loves you—loves you as I do— loves you for yourself!" said he. "For both

your sakes,——for all our sakes——better that
the intimacy should end."

And it *has* ended.   No communication ever
passed between us from the hour of my marriage——except a distant bow when we met in
the world——until this unlucky ball.   Why——
why was I so bewildered by my vanity as to
overlook, even for a moment, the prohibition
of my husband !——

Herbert is at all times one of the finest
young men in England.   But never did I see
him look so noble and distinguished as in the
dress of a Knight of the Golden Fleece, which
he wore on the present occasion.   And yet,
I never saw him so little like himself !——Instead of his usual grave reserve, his head appeared as much turned as my own by the
levity of the night.   There was an affectation
of triumph in his air as he took me from my
husband's arm and led me to my place opposite the queen and court.——

I fancied——it *might* be fancy——that a murmur of general admiration arose when the
full-toned orchestra struck up for our minuet.

Of course I only shared the applause with Mary Herbert and my sisters-in-law. But at the moment, my vain heart suggested every eye as fixed upon myself; under which impression I grew sadly confused.

My confusion, indeed, must have been evident to all. For Lord Herbert instantly began to whisper words of encouragement: and the first time the figure of the minuet enabled him to take my hand, he had the audacity to press it, precisely as when, in our days of courtship, he made me the offer of his own.

But mine was not, as then, withdrawn. Without making a scene, it would have been impossible ; and every time the figure brought us together, in spite of the indignant and reproving expression of my countenance, his offence was renewed. In the last figure, when the cavalier takes both the hands of his partner, he seized upon mine with an ardour and impetuosity which, I feared, must be as perceptible to the whole room as it was embarrassing to myself.

I resolved, of course, the moment the concluding curtsey of the minuet set me at liberty, to join my sisters-in-law, and go in search of Arthur, without exchanging either a look or word with my presumptuous partner. But how was this to be done?——Lady Sophia and her sister were dancing with favourite partners, with whom they instantly made off to the tea-room; and even Lady Mary was too much engrossed by her handsome Highland cavalier, to do more than reply to my inquiries " whether she had seen Lord Trevor?" that he was " waltzing in the gallery with Countess Dietrichstein!"——

She spoke with an arch smile; as if aware that I had been taxing Trevor, the preceding evening, with his excessive admiration of the Austrian ambassadress.

What was to be done?——*There* I stood, in the centre of that immense ball-room, looking very awkward and very silly; *embarrassée de ma contenance,* as the French say. On finding a second royal minuet about to commence, not daring to cross the room alone, I was only too glad to accept Lord Herbert's arm to lead me to my place.

But where *was* my place? Every seat was occupied, and Lord Trevor dancing!—Provoking was the smile with which Lord Herbert pointed out this to my notice, as he quietly mingled with the throng moving towards the refreshment-room, as though it were our only resource, and I had no choice but to be acquiescent.

The only persons near me with whom I was acquainted, were the Duchess of St. Michaels, Lady Castlemoat's sister, who has always received me with the utmost coldness, and on the present occasion chilled me almost to tears by her stiff bow; and two or three young men who smiled significantly at Herbert as we passed. I even made a second attempt to join Lady Sophia, on finding my arm fondly pressed under that of my partner. But she not only shrugged her shoulders as I approached her, but whispered something to Lord Edwin, on whose arm she was leaning, about *manque d'usage*, which, I am certain, applied to *me*.

What was I to do?——I now see clearly what
I *ought* to have done.   But the intoxication of
the hour prevailed.   Stung to the soul by the
neglect of my husband and the impertinence of
his family, I nerved my courage,——I subdued
my repugnance,——and resolved to act as I had
seen others act under similar circumstances.

" They have chosen me to be Lady Barbara
for to-night, and Lady Barbara I will be!"
thought I, still straining my head to overlook
the crowd, in the vain hope that Arthur
might be following us through the throng.
——Alas!——not a vestige of him!——From a distance, the air of the waltz in which he was still
engaged pursued me, like a guilty thought;
till, piqued and mortified, I went and sat down
in a corner of the refreshment-room with Lord
Herbert; so faint, that I could hardly stand.

At length, I discerned afar off the magnificent emeralds of the countess; and though
the intervening crowd prevented my seeing
who was her partner, the expression of Lord
Herbert's face, who was at that moment addressing me, told me plainer than words that

it was no other than my husband. God forgive
me!——But I could scarcely breathe!——

While waiting for the carriage, that evening, to repair to Buckingham Palace, Lady
Castlemoat had amused herself with instruct-
ing me half in jest, half in earnest, in the use
of a curious old racoco fan, painted on vellum
(as it is supposed by Miguard), which she
taught me to manœuvre with the coquettish
graces which Lady Barbara (to whom it originally belonged) is said to have excelled. Now
or never was the moment to turn the lesson
to account! In the belief that Arthur was
approaching me, I strove to retaliate upon him
by replying with a hollow laugh to the compliments of Lord Herbert; flirting my gorgeous fan as I listened, with the affectation
of a practised coquette. I was heartily
ashamed of myself all the while!——But the
influence of the pink and green sacque remained paramount.

Whether my *agaceries* touched the feelings
of Arthur, I cannot guess. Those of Lord
Herbert they *certainly* did; for by degrees,

he became so *empressé* in his homage, that I
had nothing left for it but to reply in the
same tone, or abjure his acquaintance for ever.

Better if I *had!*——Instead of which, on
hearing some foolish person near me utter ex-
clamatory remarks, concerning the beauty of
the countess, I accepted his proposal that we
should join the quadrille forming in the gallery.

Oh, Lady Barbara, Lady Barbara!——If for
your sins on earth you are " Doomed for a
certain time to walk the night," or rather
dance the night, why select my poor little in-
nocent person wherein to insinuate yourself
for the performance of your pranks, to the
utter injury of my reputation,——perhaps of
my happiness for life!——

While we were dancing, Trevor came and
looked on, with an air half amused, half indignant.   But a beatiful girl was now bang-
ing upon his arm; on whom he bestowed far
more attention than on *us.*   Whom could it
be?   A *blonde*——a lovely *blonde*——with large
blue eyes!——Every thing that Arthur has so

often told me he detested!——But he seemed to detest them no longer!

I was furious. By the tremulous light of my diamond aigrette in the opposite glass, I perceived that my emotion was only too evident. Even Arthur perceived it, and was alarmed; for before the conclusion of the quadrille, he walked away.

"You are ill!" whispered Lord Herbert in the tenderest tones. "For Heaven's sake. allow me to fetch you a glass of water."

"No, no!" said I. "The heat of the room is too much for me. I will not wait for Lady Castlemoat's departure, who, as a chaperone, must stay till the end. You must do me the favour to call the carriage."

Without a word of remonstrance, he conducted me down stairs with tender care to the cloak-room; where I remained while he executed my commission. In a few minutes he hurried back; and while the cry of "Lady Trevor's carriage stops the way," resounded from the vestibule, dragged rather than led me down the steps leading into the hall, through the file of rooms in attendance; and in a moment I found myself in a carriage. Surrounded by yeomen of the guard, and startled by the shouting of the footmen in waiting, I hurried in, without noticing that it was neither my own chariot, nor Lady Castlemoat's family-coach!

It mattered little so that I was conveyed home. Lord Herbert had probably taken his sister's, seeing that mine was not to be found; and long before I reached Grosvenor Square, I was so drowned in tears—tears long repressed, and now a right welcome relief—that I had no attention to bestow on aught beside.

A thundering knock, and the steps of the carriage let down, apprised me that we had arrived; and, chiefly anxious to dry my eyes and conceal my emotions from the servants in attendance and the crowd that began to gather when the carriage stopped, I rushed into the house the moment the door was opened; nor till I was fairly in the hall did I notice the absence of the fat old family porter, or that the lamps streaming over the marble pavement, and the red baize doors thrown open for me to pass, were those of another house than that of my father-in-law!——

Starting back, I was about to explain my mistake to the astonished servants by whom I had been admitted, and return to the carriage. But already I heard it driving off!——The hall-door was closed; —— the chain up. —— And instead of servants in attendance, I saw only Lord Herbert, who must have accompanied the carriage.

Speechless with wonder and indignation, I had not power to resist when he conducted me into an apartment on the ground-floor, dimly lighted by a pair of candles, where he entreated me to repose myself. Unable to procure my carriage, and afraid lest I should become seriously indisposed at the palace, he had brought me, he said, to the house of a relative in Eaton Square, where he was every moment expecting Lady Castlemoat's carriage to fetch me away——Lord Trevor was apprised of my illness, and would doubtless soon make his appearance.——

Never shall I forget the oppression of breath that overcame me as I listened to this explanation, evidently a mere subterfuge! I tried to express my indignant feelings; but not a word could I utter.

"I do not wonder you feel indisposed, dearest Lady Trevor," said he, profiting by my embarrassment to take a seat beside me on the sofa upon which I had sunk. "It is easy for an honourable man to conceive your disgust at being required to appear in the presence of your sovereign in the costume of a woman who was a disgrace to the age in which she lived. In her lifetime, Lady Barbara Trevor was an object of terror and hatred to the obscure man on whom, in a fit of caprice, she bestowed her hereditary nobility and vast possessions. Never weary of upbraiding the unhappy soldier of fortune distinguished by her choice, her shameless immorality fully justified his repentance of the ambitious marriage which served only to confer nobility on his heirs.

"And was such a woman," he continued,

modulating his voice to a more tender key, as he endeavoured to take my hand, "was such a woman the only model that could be found for the imitation of the gentlest, fairest, and most virtuous of her sex?"

Alarmed beyond expression, I started from my seat, and with my face crimson with shame, and with the pulses throbbing in my temples, rushed towards the door.—*It was locked!* but with supernatural strength I burst it open,—tore myself from his grasp,—and, guided by the glimmering light emitted by the half open door of the room, groped my way along a dark passage leading from the hall, where the lamps were already extinguished.

As in the corridor of a country-house, bed-rooms opened on either side. I tried several doors, but all were fast. At length, hearing the footsteps of Lord Herbert close upon me, I rushed with such force upon a door at the end of the passage that it yielded, almost with a crash, to my attack.

Judge of my amazement!—In the centre of the room stood my husband, quietly removing from his shoulder the Order of the Bath he had worn that evening in the costume of Sir Harry Chamberlain.

"What, in the name of Heaven, Minnie, are you doing here?" cried he. But on perceiving that I was closely followed by Lord Herbert, his voice changed from an intonation of wonder to that of rage. What he uttered I dare not transcribe; but the insulting and coarse rejoinder of Lord Herbert, so much at variance with his usual deportment, seemed fully to justify the increasing fury of my husband.

At any other moment, my first impulse would have been to throw myself into the arms of Arthur and denounce the treachery by which I had been misguided: but in his present mood I dared not. Both he and Lord Herbert were actuated by sentiments so strange, so ungovernable, so frantic, that I trembled on perceiving that my husband still wore his sword, and that the hand of Lord Herbert was on the hilt of his blade.

How is it that at such moments some

women become endowed with instinctive eloquence, more powerful than strength; while others remain meek, weak, and helpless—helpless as I was, as I stood, speechless and wringing my hands, between those who were thirsting for each other's blood!—

In another moment that blood was drawn. On my husband's haughty command to his rival to quit the room, Lord Herbert rushed upon him like a madman. Not a step could I stir to interpose between them.—At that crisis of horror, had millions of human lives depended upon it, I could not have uttered a single shriek.

I heard the clash of swords—I saw the bright steel flash, as Lord Herbert, blind with rage.... But no, I cannot write it! In another second I was on the floor, beside the bleeding body of my husband, imploring him, like the distracted Belvidera, to speak to me, though it were but a word—though it were but a *curse*,— and pressing my lips to his clammy forehead—to his cold cheek—to his fixed and lustreless eyes.

A deep, deep sob burst from my oppressed heart, as suddenly a warmer touch apprised me that my trembling hands were clasped in those of another. Believing myself to be again assailed by Lord Herbert, I snatched them furiously away ; when, lo ! my ears were greeted by a joyous, ringing laugh, and on unclosing my eyes, which I had averted from the scene of horror, they rested upon my unfortunate maid, standing by my bedside, holding over her arm the pink and green sacque, full trimmed, and ready to be tried on !

Oh, what a joy to find myself in my cheerful bedroom at Trevor Court, with the sun of a May morning shining full into the room !

"I have been waiting breakfast for you these ten minutes," cried Arthur, pressing to his lips the hand I no longer withdrew. "But I will not ask you what detained you.—Wilson tells me she has been so busy finishing your costume that she has allowed you to oversleep yourself. What a shocking nightmare you have had !"

"Take away that dress, and never let me

hear the name of Lady Barbara Trevor again,"
cried I, unable to repress my tears of self-
gratulation on finding my terrible ordeal only
a dream. "You *must*,—indeed you *must*,
find some pretext for our absenting ourselves
from the ball !"

" But my mother—think of my father and
mother's indignation !" remonstrated Arthur,
who had been examining with provoking com-
placency my beautiful dress.

Even *that* consideration, however, did not
suffice to reconcile me to the pink and green
sacque. And a few days afterwards, I was
enabled to suggest a pretext for remaining
quietly in the country, which the whole family
kindly admitted to be valid. All my previous
ennui, all my restless nights were accounted
for.—"An heir to the house of all the Trevors"
is in prospect.

" Country air and perfect tranquillity " are
luckily recommended by the family oracle in
whom Lady Castlemoat has implicit confidence; and though I have had sufficient self-
command to intreat that Arthur will profit

by the invitation with which he had been honoured, he has decided (in *my* opinion as judiciously as kindly) that he should find no pleasure in the royal ball, now that the Red Riband has no chance of companionship with the pink and green sacque.

May my slumbers never again be troubled by so frightful a dream as my

VISION OF THE ROYAL BALL !——

END OF THE JOURNAL.

AN ACCOUNT OF A CREDITOR.

People plead guilty to *duns* :——the word carries an air of defiance with it which they fancy becoming. But few like to talk of their *creditors* ;——a name which, by conveying a consciousness of legal responsibility, conveys also a wound to their self-love.

Yet, from the moment that, by drawing breath, we incur the debt of nature, to that when the bell, tolling over our remains, conveys pecuniary liability to our inheritors, life is a series of indebtments. Thrice happy the man who sleeps solvent upon his pillow. But scarcely less pitiful the wretch who lays his head there absolutely debtless ;——untrusted either because untrustworthy, or because unwilling to accord credit in return !

The pre-eminence of Great Britain among nations is ascribed by the farthest-sighted philosophers to the magnitude of her national debt; and but for the stimulus of private liabilities, where would be the best works of the best authors,——the best pictures of the best artists,——the best articles of the best magazines? The high-mettled scribbler starts off at speed on the slightest spur of a dun; and the Scotch novels are in a great measure the works of the creditors of Scott.

A gentleman with whom I recently became acquainted supplied me not alone with the foregoing theory of philosophy, but with the following narrative in support of his system—" My parents," said he, " died when I was a schoolboy, having been what is called ' unfortunate;' and I was bequeathed to the guardianship of a crabbed uncle, with so small a patrimony, that I and *it* together seemed scarcely worth the trouble of looking after. To me, however, those three thousand pounds appeared to contain a mine of wealth; and, in my vague notions of independence, I scorned all mention of articles to attorneys, clerkships in counting-houses, apprenticeships to apothecaries already smitten with the wild desire of becoming a man of wit and pleasure about town!

According to the privilege of uncles well to do in the world, *mine* called me a fool. But he had said as much of my parents when ruined by speculation; and in his house I had already been taught to understand the approbrious word, according to a lexicon especially Great British, as the synonym of " poor." But believing myself to be both wealthy and wise——that is, being so great a fool as to judge myself capable of achieving wealth through my own wisdom,—I snapped my fingers at my uncle, and betook myself to the lean and hungry occupation of polite scholarship.

Like other enthusiastic lads to whom parental coercion has been wanting, I fancied myself a man of genius. Pactolus seemed waiting to flow through my hands; and it needed only a stroke of my poetic wand to convert the waters of oblivion into claret and champagne.

The first thing that flowed through my
hands was of course my small fortune.   Till
I attained my majority, I lived upon tick;
and the first act of my first year of discretion
being to discharge to the last doit my obligations, established a credit much *to* my
credit, and little to my advantage.

Convinced that the efforts of my pen would
enable me to strike a future balance as readily
as in the present instance, by inditing a draft
upon my uncle's *hauteur*, I persisted in the
personal engagements which had converted
my inheritance into a four years' income ;—
my tragedy, my comedy, my epic, my farce,
my annual, my magazine, being destined to
metamorphose all future creditors into my
most obedient humble servants.

Alas! the only transformation I ever
witnessed in them, was from creditors into
duns.   Perceiving me to be a man of honour
by the readiness with which I discharged the
illegal obligations of my minority, they set
me down as soft, and became proportionably
hard.   By degrees mistrusted, eventually

trusted no longer, there came to be a sort of poetic license in the cut and texture of my garments, such as constitutes in itself an act of bankruptcy.

Still, I was young and sanguine. As I ascended my lodgings story above story, I was only soaring a poetical flight. I thought of Milton, of Otway, of Goldsmith; and, comforted by prospective immortality, overlooked my mortal necessities. Moreover, an occasional sparkle of gold-dust on the surface redoubled my faith in the latent mines below. The first time I pocketed a guinea as the guerdon of two months' hard labour in leading articles for a weekly paper, I beheld myself the founder of a future Abbotsford —a baronet—a member of parliament!

At that moment, indeed, I even forgot my creditors. But my creditors, alas.! did not forget *me!* With all my flights, I had only attained a third pair of stairs; and steep and rickety as they were, one might have fancied them smooth as the verses of Rogers, and carpeted with Axminster, so pleasant appeared

the ascent to every savage in whose books I
had inscribed myself pending the triumphs of
my own. It seemed a mall to the brutes—a
ring, a *Cours la reine*, a *Prater*, a *Chiaja*—
for their daily exercise and delectation. My
bell had a silver sound in their ears;—and
they came both " single spies," and " in
battalions."

I paid—when I could,—and at length promised to pay—when I could : an expression
they seemed to hold too vague and figurative;
for most of them (probably for the pleasure
of possessing my autograph as a literary
man) required me to say as much, and sometimes a little more, upon paper.

Now, my autograph happened to be precisely that of my crabbed uncle; so that he
became, for reasons of his own, desirous of
withdrawing it from circulation. He was,
therefore, at the trouble of collecting the first
series of these offsprings of my pen ; apprizing me, at the same time, that my next
performance of the same nature might be in
the hands of the attorneys, and the unfortu-

nate author in quod till the day of judgment, for any effort he would make towards the redemption of either.

In former days, it was held a christianly thing to release captives from thrall; and kings on their deathbeds, and ladies fair in pain or peril, used to make vows of ransom for so many victims of the Moors. But neither kings nor countesses of modern times extend their tender mercies towards the victims of sheriff's officers; and I accordingly determined that, whatever bills might be brought against me, I would give none in return. I was beginning to understand the value of my own autograph.

This resolution only increased my influx of visitors. The sneaks crowding to write their names in the porter's book of a royal giver of fêtes, are not more assiduous than the little knot of uncrediting creditors who daily assured me that they were tired of having reminded me of their claims—as though I were not equally tired of hearing of them!

Custom has appropriately assigned the

office of dunning to the most disagreeable moment of the year;——the moment when its two ends meet, though our own do *not*;——the days when " daylight dies" so soon after its birth, that it scarcely seems worth while for it to have come into the world;——and when, as we emerge from our cheerless houses into the chilly atmosphere,

> The bravest holds his breath
> For a time !

In those Christmas days of darkness and desolation, the sound of single knocks is great in the land. Parallelogrammatic letters, wafer-sealed and unsightly, make their appearance at every door. Not a tyro of a clerk but seems to be learning to draw in figures. Saints and sinners unite in bidding their fellow-creatures L.S.D.——d ; and, knowing our inability before they ask, and their ignorance in asking, request us, " at our earliest convenience," to settle their small accounts. The world seems bent, in short, upon prolonging by weariness of spirit the brevity of the shortest day of the year!

Among mine enemies (at the period when I was beginning to comprehend the identity between an enemy and a creditor) was a certain rich man, who swore he was a very poor one,—Jonas Cox by name, and a tailor by nature. Yes, by nature; for he was born a tailor, a chip of the old shop-board, a Snip of many generations. There had been as many Coxes in his cabbagery as Guelphs upon the throne of Great Britain. He was Cox VI., of Poland Street; had come into the world cross-legged, and was likely to exhibit his cross-bones in the same sartorial bearings.

Jonas Cox, I blush to own, was my family tailor. Though his cut was such as fully to justify my cutting *him*, in recalling to mind how he had admeasured me for my schoolboy jackets aforetime, and annually wasted upon my crabbed uncle the assurance (so sweet in the ears of parents) that I was " growing a fine young gentleman," when I grew to be merely a *fine* gentleman, I remembered the

days of my youth and Jonas Cox—eschewed
Stultz, Burghart, and Buckmaster, Cooke, Ink-
son, and Curlewis,——and left my measures to
the exclusive care of Poland Street, as her
Majesty those of Government to the hands of
Sir Robert Peel. So long as I could be classed
among the good customers of Jonas, I was
" dressed," as dinners are promised at
suburban taverns, " on the shortest notice ;"
and let me add, as the said dinners are *not*, on
the longest credit.

Among the accounts discharged with interest on the attainment of my majority, was
one of Cox VI.th's, which for length, if shred
into tailor's measures, would have " put a
girdle round about the earth," or the waist
of Daniel Lambert. The amount of the
stamp for the receipt in full would now
afford me a week's board and lodging ! Jonas
Cox was, accordingly, one of those who
waited longest subsequently before he requested the favour of my autograph ; and it
was through the importunities of the family-
tailor to my uncle that my signature for once

held good, to be consigned to dishonour for evermore.

But on the Christmas ensuing, Jonas saw fit to deliver his bill as he had formerly delivered his suits—at the shortest notice;—ay, and to deliver it with " damnable iteration." Lest I should mistake his meaning, the second and third reading of the bill expressed only " to bill delivered'—*call* and deliver being the watchword of one's thieves of creditors, as *stand* and deliver used to be of the footpads of more heroic times.

At length, to this single line of argument were appended half a dozen more, requesting my immediate attention to the same ; receiving no answer to which, Jonas probably concluded, like the belle of a country town concerning some militia captain, that my " attentions meant nothing."

His next missive announced a visit from his clerk, who called, and called, and called again ; and I, though " not at home" to his calls, of course forgot to return the visit.

Then came a letter of orthography so

much more impeachable than the preceding
ones, that it was plain the old goose had
taken quill in hand to defend his own cause;
for he assured me it " would not suit him to
whait any longer."

Next followed a lawyer's letter!

Before it reached my lodgings, I was hundreds of miles away; gathering up a small
inheritance from a maiden aunt, which enabled
me to satisfy Cox VI. by a large instalment,
and for nearly a year ensuing, relieved me
from further mention of his name.

Last Christmas, however, there arrived, in
the well-known clerkly handwriting, " To
balance of account——," with the superaddi-
tion of the cost of a suit of nephew's mourning, which still constitutes the customary suit
of rusty black of my quotidian wear.

Mr. Jonas Cox, it appeared, had retired
from business. His riches had been increasing in the same proportion as my poverty;
and he was now the proprietor of a charming
villa, Number 3, Elysium Road, Maida Hill.
Unluckily for me, in arranging his dissolution

of partnership with his son, Cox VII., what were insolently called the bad debts of the firm fell to the share of the old man—among the rest, mine! To collect these outstanding claims seemed to have become the recreation of his leisure. It was a pastime to him, after counting the numbers of sprigs on his Michaelmas daisies in Elysium Row, and listening all the morning to the toll of the adjacent burying-ground, to take the omnibus to town, and hunt up, in their tranquil retreats, the thirty-seven unfortunate wretches whose names still figured in his schedule.

They were his game—his bagged foxes—the sport of his new gentility—the memento of his former occupation. For Cox VII. had a touch of Philip the Second in him, and did not care to have the abdicated emperor resume his sceptre in Poland Street, *i. e.* his scissors; and repulsed in his old workshop,

> Without the power to fill again
> The desert gap that caused his pain,

by the concoction of new measures, or the hatching of another goose, Jonas could only become the ninth part of a man again, by the perusal and reperusal of those accursed old bills; and not only " whaiting" *for* them, but waiting *with* them upon his debtors.

I have reason to think I was peculiarly favoured. As I said before, my lodgings were high,—high as his demands;— and by the time the old man had panted his way up to my door, Christian charity demanded that I should offer him a chair for the recovery of his breath, pending the recovery of his money. After due discussion of the "to pay or not to pay" part of my abilities, he was about to enter into that of their literary value; first, talking of his own books, secondly, of mine. But he had known me since I was breeched; and was privileged.

Nor was the privilege unappreciated; for instead of Christmas remaining the exclusive period for persecution, his visits beset me all the year round. The finest day in June was not secure against the intrusions of Jonas Cox. Presuming on the indulgence he had shown me, it became an understood thing between

us that, though steeped to the lips in poverty
and printer's ink, I was never to be denied to
the retired tailor.   He had acquired one-hun-
dred-and-twenty-seven pounds' worth of right
to come and sit in the sunshine of my spirit,
converting it into carefulness and gloom.
He loved to talk to me of my parents and
their troubles ; and how little they had ever
expected their only son would come to live
in a garret, scribbling for bread.   And then he
would take out his silver snuff-box, or wipe
his unctuous brows with a motley bandana, as
he added that " my uncle was getting stricken
in years.   But he feared I should be never
the better for his death ; his fortune being notoriously divided between public charities and
the charity that begun at home in the person of his robust housekeeper."

I bore it all.   Though arsenic is dirt-cheap,
and prussic acid far from ruinous, and Jonas
Cox would have gratefully accepted any refreshment I saw fit to offer him, whether liquid
or substantial, I refrained.—I looked upon
the old wretch as a species of materialized

conscience,— an embodied remorse;—a monitor or tormentor entailed upon me by my expensive habits!——

At length one autumn morning, when, soon after his arrival in my poor chamber, "drizzly rain did fall," rendering it impossible for him to regain his omnibus without being soaked to his unmacintoshed skin, I saw that my day was sacrificed, and with it a brilliant article, which had been spirting forth from my pen at the moment of his arrival, and which his doleful family allusions checked in a moment. Transpierced by the acupunctuation of the tailor's needle, my balloon had fallen from the clouds!

"*Tu me lo pagherai!*" muttered I——(as the tailor had often probably muttered to himself touching his bill while ascending my creaking stairs!)——"You shall furnish me with a substitute."

It was only to transcribe from the caitiff's own lips one of the anecdotes of my thirty-six brother-martyrs, with which he was in the habit of favouring me. I am perhaps investing his story with the colouring of my own imagination. But I remember I had a hard matter to gulp down my tears while he narrated to me the following adventure.

"Yesterday was a mighty pleasant day to me," observed the old tailor, as he sat slowly chafing his knees beside my fire. "Yesterday, sir, I recovered a debt even more desperate than yours; a matter of forty pounds, which I had given up as a bad job.——Much such a case, indeed, as your own; a family I had worked for, partly for love, partly for money, these fifty years; I and my father, Jacob Cox, afore me.

"People well to do in the world were those Fosters! The grandfather, a rich merchant, with a substantial house in Bedford Row, and everything comfortable about him; so that it was a pleasure when his family coach and fat coachhorses, looking like emblems of peace and plenty, stopped at my door.——I loved to measure his men for their liveries! There was a world of good living, sir, in their dimensions. The body coachman and gouty old footman must have weighed together nigh forty stone.——

" He had two sons, had the old gentleman
—likely little fellows as you'd wish to see,
in their sugarloaf-buttoned jackets, and nan-
keen trousers; and by the time I had to
stand on tiptoe while trying them on, young
men of what is called the highest promise.
Old Foster couldn't be worth less than a hundred thousand pounds; and as he had only a
couple of daughters to provide for in addition
to his handsome sons, (one, at least, of whom
was sure of his share in the house of business,)
they might be considered as easy for life. *I*,
God knows, considered them so; and was
always careful to comply with their whims,
and be punctual to their orders. Besides, they
were good-looking youths, who did honour to
my shop. You may not think it of much
moment, sir, but I can tell you we tailors love
to work for a man who is as well made as
his coat!

" You see the fat footman and fat coachman
were apt to gossip of their master's affairs,
when they came about their plush waistcoats

and velveteens, as servants, whether fat or lean, are apt to do ; more especially about Christmas time, when the family accounts being sent in, family tradesmen are obliged to stand a glass or two as a token of respect to the servants' hall ; and it was the opinion of old Foster's people that he would divide the property between his two sons, leaving the eldest to succeed him in his business.

" The young men, however, were not equally favourites with the old servants. There was no end of the faults found with Master Harry, or, as he was now beginning to be called, ' Mister Henry !'——Mister Henry kept them up late at nights ;——Mister Henry was late of mornings ;——Mister Henry required more brushing of coats and polishing of boots than any ten Mister Henries in the land. Mister Henry professed that he would sooner walk ten miles in the rain than undergo the penance of the family coach ; and Mister Henry had even been heard to speak disparagingly of the home-brewed of Bedford Row !——whereas the elder-born, the hope of

the house, was a model young man——early to
bed and early to rise — unimpeachable in
morals, and so far from giving three pair of
boots a day to be varnished, much addicted
to gaiters.   Yet such is the perversity of
human nature, sir, that Henry was ten to one
the favourite.   The fat footman used to per-
jure his precious soul in trying to conceal
from the old gentleman the indecent hours of
the young scapegrace !

"John Foster, the elder brother, did his
best, as perhaps in duty bound, to prevent his
father from being deceived on such points.
For it was doubtless for Henry's good, that
he should be daily reproved;   and though it
was likely enough to banish him from the old
gentleman's good books to learn that he was
getting pretty deep into other people's, his
brother took care that the amount of his
debts should be no secret in Bedford Row.

" Don't suspect me, sir, of having aided or
abetted this.   1 protest to you that, from the
time the young gentleman lived upon an
allowance, many was the Christmas I let pass

without doing more than add up in my books the account of Mr. Henry. For I knew well enough, from the hints of the fat footman, that if ever so much sent in, it wouldn't be paid; so where was the use of bothering him? The family bill was, as usual, duly settled. John Foster used to pay ready money for his goods, for the sake of discount; and with such steady customers in the house, the less need to fret at the backwardness of the younger son.

" And to say the truth, like the old servants, I felt something of a weakness in favour of that young man! He was so good-looking, so affable, so pleasant, he had such a way with him, as the saying is, that all his little faults were readily excused. For, as bad a paymaster as he was, and though I seldom sent him home a coat that he didn't tell my foreman my quizzical cut made him the laughing-stock of his acquaintance, I liked *his* sauciness full as well as the dryness of the ready-money chap, who took discount, and gave neither praise nor blame.

"My wife used often to scold me, when she saw how Henry Foster's bill was running up; and swore she'd have it made out and sent in to his father.   But I pacified her by assuring her he would pay me in the lump; and bade her take care how she slew the old goose in Bedford Row, for the sake of a few golden eggs.

"However, in time, the young jackanapes made me ashamed of my own indulgence; for, (will you believe it?) he had the face to come to me one evening, pale as ashes and with scarcely breath to speak, and entreat me to put my name to a bill for him!   He had got into trouble, and assured me it would ruin him with his father if the circumstance transpired.   A pretty joke, truly, wasn't it, for the name of Jonas Cox of Poland Street to be essential to the credit of Mr. Henry Foster, of Great St. Helen's and Bedford Row?"——

"You complied, then, with his request?" said I, in some amazement.

"If I did," rejoined the old snip, (apparently alarmed lest I should ground expectations upon his weakness,) " the matter occurred five-and-twenty years ago, or more,—and, thank goodness, I am older and wiser now!—Even then, I wouldn't have had my wife know that I'd put my foot into it to the tune of three hundred pounds, for double the money!"

" You lost it, then ?—They came upon you for the amount of the bill?"—

" On the contrary, some days before 'twas due, Harry Foster walked into my shop,—had his account added up before him,—and without so much as examining the items, gave me a cheque upon his banker for the sum total of the whole!

" ' Old Cox,' said he, ' you are a trump!' —or words to that effect—' The assistance you rendered me was invaluable, and I can't better prove my gratitude than by wiping off old scores. I've had a run of luck, old fellow, and look upon *you* as the origin of my change of fortune.'

" And he literally threw a guinea to my

son Elias, sir, then a little boy in petticoats,
playing with the pattern-book in the corner
of the shop.

" You may believe how I crowed over my
wife, as I wrote ' Settled' at the foot of the
long account about which she had jeered me
so often.

" And now, sir, she began to jeer me,
forsooth that, having lost my debtor, I should
certainly lose my customer.   No such thing !
Mr. Henry gave me an order not a week
afterwards ; and found only half the fault he
used to do, seeing that he was in better
humour with himself and the world.

" He was, in fact, in the best of humour
with himself.   For he was in love, sir, and
fancied himself beloved in return : and few
things put a young man in finer conceit with
his merits.   I could see, whenever he entered
my shop, that he seemed to walk two inches
taller than formerly ; nor could he forbear
casting a glance in the swing-glass as he went
by, which before he had never noticed.   All
this did not surprise me ; for I had learned

from the fat footman, that instead of coming in late of nights, Mr. Henry had ceased to come in at all !

"One day, my wife accosted me before I had crossed the threshold, on my return from waiting upon a customer,——(and now I call to mind, sir, the customer was neither more nor less than your own good uncle,)——she accosted me, I say, with an exclamation of ' Here's a pretty kettle of fish !——What 'll you say now, Cox, to the doings of your paragon in Bedford Row !'——

" ' Mr. Henry ?' cried I, aghast, ' What has happened to him ? What has he been about ?'

" ' It has happened to him to be turned out o' doors by his father !' replied my wife. ' And right enough too !—A young gentleman of *his* prospects to go and marry a play-actress !—Ay ! you may well hold up your hands and eyes—'tis no more than every other soul has done belonging to him.—But all too late !—The mischief's done ; and I find from the Bedford Row coachman, (who's been

sitting here as down in the mouth as though
he'd buried his wife,) that the moment the
news was carried to old Foster by his precious
son John, the old man gave his maledic-
tion to Henry, forbade him the house, and,
what was worse than all, scratched his name
out of his will!'

" On inquiry, all this news, strange as it
was, proved true. The clandestine marriage
of the young man had been discovered
through the interference of his brother ; and
old Foster, whose opposition might have been
overcome perhaps had his son shown confidence in his indulgence, could not forgive
having been imposed upon. As my wife
announced, he had cursed and disinherited
his favourite child !

" I couldn't help feeling a little curious to
learn how the poor young fellow was getting
on in his troubles. But when I inquired in
Bedford Row, nobody knew a word concerning him, and few had courage to mention his
name. For my part, I didn't like to stir.
Having a small account against him, I was

afraid Mr. Henry might fancy, if he found that Cox the tailor was inquiring after him, that I wanted payment of my bill ; so I let months, and even the year slip on, without so much as asking a question. Yet, I vow to goodness, I was almost as much vexed as if I had caught out one of my children in a lie or a theft, whenever I thought of that fine gentlemanly young man having thrown himself away on a play-acting miss ;—some impudent, ranting jade, who had trapped him afore he knew what he was about.

" It was nigh two years after the bad news first reached me, that I received a note from Mr. Henry, begging me to call, when convenient, at a number he gave me in an obscure street, bordering on Long Acre. Poor fellow ! A momentary expectation which had beset me, on seeing his handwriting, that I was going to receive the amount of my small bill against him disappeared in a moment.— Poverty breathed in every line of that short note.

" Nevertheless, I was not an atom prepared

for what met my eyes on entering his lodgings.
The sitting-room was much about the size of
this, sir, opening into a bed-room, which was
also a nursery, as the sitting-room served
equally the purpose of a kitchen.　Yet
wretched as it all was for a gentleman
brought up like Mr. Henry, I promise you
there was nothing unsightly in the arrange-
ments. All was neat, clean, and orderly. The
little cradle placed beside the tidy white bed
looked so cozy, and the few books ranged on
the console, and the writing-desk on the
table, reminded me so much of the Master
Harry of former days, (in whose handsome
bed-room in Bedford Row, reading and
writing materials always had their place,)
that, strange as it might seem to find the
opulent young man reduced to such needi-
ness, I never a moment doubted I had found
my way right.

　" And yet, when I came to see him, that is,
when he made his appearance out of the bed-
room to meet me, his person was ten times
more altered than his condition!　I could

scarce have believed the lapse of three years
able to trace so many lines in a human face.
His hair was thinned ;——his smile (for he *did*
smile at seeing me) was ghastly !——Still, he
tried to speak cheerfully, and hailed me as
' Jonas, my old boy !' as he used, in his
better days. But there was something painful in the distance between those gay words
and the hollow voice in which they were
uttered. For my part, I tried to answer him
more respectfully than ever.

" He made me sit down——but that he was
always used to do when I waited upon him
in Bedford Row, if not ready to attend to
me on my arrival ; and though, perhaps,
I had better have held my tongue, I could
not forbear telling him how it made my
old heart ache to find him in so poor a place.

" ' A *poor*, but not a sad one, I promise you !'
was his cheerful reply ; though the smile he
had called up to welcome me had already
vanished. ' I have treasures here, Jonas, I
never possessed in Bedford Row,——treasures
such as any man might be proud of !'

" And immediately he glided back into the inner room, and brought back in his arms a beautiful boy of two years old,——one of those curly-headed, blue-eyed creatures, that painters put into their pictures, and which one sees so seldom in real flesh and blood. The child put out one of its dimpled hands towards me at his father's desire, but only nestled the closer to him for seeing a stranger in the room ; and the round rosy smiling face leaning against the countenance of the careworn man, served to make its leanness more apparent.

" ' Baby's asleep !' lisped the little fellow into his father's ear ; upon which Mr. Henry hastily explained to me that on my entrance he was sitting in the other room with his wife, who had only been confined a fortnight.

" ' I make a capital nurse, Jonas, as you may see,' continued he, again attempting a ghastly smile. 'One never does anything half so well as the accomplishments one practises of one's own accord. And God knows, I ought to exert myself as a nurse during

Emma's sickness; for, when well, not a finger will she ever allow me to stir in aid of our little household. I did not choose an heiress, Cox, my boy, as my brother John has done, —nor a fine lady, as my sisters wished me. But, if a frugal, laborious, virtuous, forbearing, tender wife be a crown of rubies, I have got it, if ever man *had!*"

"It was a pleasure to hear him speak so; and the neatness and orderliness of his poor home certainly said much in confirmation of his words. Still, I could not forbear inquiring why he made no advances towards a reconciliation with his family.

"'*Advances?*' cried he. 'Can you suppose that, with these dear ones around me wanting all but bread, I have not humiliated myself to the utmost? I have submitted to be repulsed, insulted, threatened; and when, on my last application to my father for even a trifling assistance, he sent me word that my wife had better go on the stage again, and earn a maintenance for her brats—then, *then* indeed, I swore as great an oath as my father had already sworn never to see my face again, that rather should my children starve before my face than I would address myself further to my family.'

" ' It is all Mr. John's doing !' muttered I, incautiously.

" ' My brother and sisters have not stood my friends !' replied young Foster. 'But had there been in my father's heart any real tenderness towards me, would the fact of my choosing a wife otherwise than he desired, (more especially when he came to know that wife as all that is truest and best in womanly nature,) determine him to cast off the son of his loins?—No, no, Cox, my boy!—My father always preferred John. John's sober, business-like ways, and sneaking submission, engrossed his affections; and I am reaping the harvest on't. The old gentleman wanted an excuse for leaving his fortune to my brother; so as to keep up the magnitude of the house of business.'

" I suppose my young friend discovered by the expression of my countenance that I was puzzling myself how to bring out an offer of such poor assistance as I was able to render ; for he suddenly started up with a change of countenance, and, while depositing the child on the hearthrug, exclaimed,

" ' Not that I am in *immediate* necessity ! I have work in hand that will place me comparatively at ease——copying, for a house in the city'——(and he pointed to several quires of MS. lying beside his open desk)——' which, when finished and paid for, will make me rich for months to come. It would have been done a week ago, but for poor Emma's illness. She has no other nurse ; and though requiring less attendance than woman ever did, the children constantly call me from my desk.'

" I could scarce find courage and words to express a wish that he would at least permit me to advance him a portion of the forthcoming payment.

" ' No, no, no !' cried he ; ' I have no need of any such act of kindness, which I nevertheless feel as it deserves. The worst is

over now.   We have struggled through the
hardest time.   Emma is safe, and I have
scarcely a care remaining' — and again he
smiled one of those terrible smiles.   ' The
service I *really* want you to do me, Cox,'
continued he, ' is to make me a good warm
frieze coat, that will enable me to sit up without a fire these bitter nights.   I write late—
I am *forced* to write late—and the remains of
my wardrobe, such as they are, afford nothing
solid enough for my purpose.   You used to
work for a fine gentleman, Cox, and worked
accordingly.   Now, you must give me something strong and coarse, that will resist time
and weather.   But 'tis not the *article* of
which I am in fear—tell me—are you afraid
to trust me ?'

 " I replied that I was very much hurt at
his asking the question, and, without further
words, went straight home, and set my men
to work so close, that next morning I was
able to take home to Mr. Henry the warmest
and best turned-out beaver wrappingcoat that
ever you set eyes upon ! (I wish I'd such

another beside me this very moment, to keep me from the rain on my way to the omnibus!) And that wasn't all. With my wife's help, sir, I managed to turn out a little greatcoat of fine cloth for the boy, and asked his father's acceptance of it in such terms that he couldn't be affronted; reminding him of the guinea he had thrown to Elias when playing in the corner of my shop. I thought there were tears in Mr. Henry's sunken eyes as I alluded to the matter. But he said, in low voice, he remembered nothing about it.

" However, he showed his thankfulness in a way that pleased me, for he led me into the sick room where his wife was sitting up for the first time with her infant in her arms, looking so pale and delicate that it seemed wonderful she could be alive; and ' Emma, my dear,' said he, bending down to her, ' this is old Cox, of whom you have heard me speak so often, as having stood my friend in the first scrape I ever got into.——He has been kind enough to make this warm little coat for Henry.——See, it fits as though you had made it yourself!'

" And partly through weakness, and partly through the pleasure of seeing her beautiful child so respectably dressed, the poor thing burst into tears.   So, while her husband was pacifying her, and removing the babe from her arms into the cradle, I slipped down stairs, and left them together.——I can't tell you, sir, what a heartache I carried with me out of that house !

" For me, Jonas Cox, a poor tailor working for the maintenance of his own family, to think of rendering assistance to the son of an old hunks with five thousand a year, would have been ridiculous.   So I set about considering how I could get some of these matters made known to Mr. Foster, who, I felt sure, was partly kept in the dark.   I bethought me, therefore, of the old coachman, and portly footman, who always seemed to love Master Harry as though he were a child of their own; and away I trudged to Bedford Row, to see what could be done toward reaching the ear of their master. Bless your soul! the knocker was tied up. The old gentleman had undergone a dreadful operation for some inward tumour, (I think, from his conduct, it must have been in his heart!) and wasn't to be spoken to even by the surgeons.——Next day, sir, he died!"

"Leaving, of course, the will by which your young friend was disinherited?"

"Worse and worse! (that there should be such men in the world and call themselves Christians!) leaving his whole fortune to his eldest son, and annuities to his daughters——on the express condition that neither of them rendered the smallest assistance to their brother Henry;—in which case, the property was to be paid over, by trustees appointed for the purpose, to create a new ward in one of the city hospitals;——unless (for, unrelenting as he was, old Foster seemed disposed to leave a loophole for Henry's escape,) unless he chose to break off the infamous connexion he had formed, and resume his place in his brother's house of business; when he was to receive an annuity of eight hundred per annum, with the power of settling three thereof upon the actress and her offspring."

" It would appear, then, that the old gentleman did not believe in the reality of their marriage ?"

" John Foster took care of that! The father's severity had purported only to bring his son to terms, and he actually died, believing that, in time, Harry would grow weary of his disreputable habits, and, having secured a provision for his mistress, end his days in decent competence. The cunning brother of course knew better; having so dictated the phrasing of his father's will as to render compliance on Henry's part as impossible as any concession on his own. By an act of fiendish foresight, therefore, the young man's ruin was irretrievable !"

Just at that moment, a brightening, or rather diminished gloom of the atmosphere, induced old Cox to toddle to the window, in hopes the weather was clearing up. Not an umbrella was perceptible, and he accordingly began to button up his coat and talk of being too late for the omnibus. I persuaded him, however, that, unless his soles were caout-chouced, the streets were still too wet to venture; and recited anecdotes of recent colds and fatal sore-throats, all occurring to hale old gentlemen of sixty-eight or there-abouts, which pinned him anew to his chair, and insured me the sequel of the melancholy story.

"You did not, I am sure, lose sight of these unfortunate people?" said I, remember-ing that, in my own case, Cox VI. exhibited a remarkable adhesiveness to the unfortunate.

"Indeed I did!" cried he, "though by no will of my own. When the time of payment of his copying came, (though in the midst of the bitterness arising from the scandalous will of his father,) Henry Foster called upon me to offer the price of the frieze coat; and a hard matter I had to make him keep back the full sum till better times."

"'Better times are coming, I trust, my kind old friend!' said he. 'By the recom-

mendation of a kinsman of my wife, I have
obtained a clerkship in a government office at
Plymouth. My salary of a hundred and
thirty pounds a-year will be riches to *us*, and
the post is a rising one. I am as happy at
this moment as the sense of ill usage at the
hands of those once nearest and dearest will
allow. But no matter; I have those, thank
God, who are nearer and dearer still; who
will never desert me—never calumniate me—
never persecute me!—And what can I want
more?'

"And he wept like a child as he took leave
of me, and thanked me for my kindness.

"Perhaps I had better have let the matter
rest so; but, for the life and soul of me, I could
not sleep till I had called at his lodgings, and
ascertained whether the little family had need
of further service on the eve of such a removal. Henry Foster was out, and I saw
only his wife.—Such a wife, sir,—such a woman! I never heard a voice like hers, or saw
such a face. There was something painful in
their sweetness;—more especially when she

talked of her husband ; and how it was impossible for her to repay his having stooped to a thing like *her;* and how, instead of being peevish with her for having caused his ruin by her fatal affection, he continued to love and serve her as though she were the greatest lady in the land !

" She did not shed a tear while she told me the melancholy history of their courtship and early struggles. But there was a sound as of tears passed in every word she uttered. And then, that lady's face seemed made of shadows. No colour, and yet it did not appear pale. I have seen wild flowers in the fields look just so—that is, so delicate of hue, that one could not say whether they were white or tinted."

I could scarcely forbear a smile at finding even old Jonas Cox grow poetical under the influence of youth and beauty. But the ex-tailor soon descended to matter of fact ;—apprized me that his offers of service were civilly declined ; that the Fosters paid all, or nearly all their liabilities on quitting London, and gradually, by instalments, satisfied the rest.

"With so many other matters to think of, I soon lost all remembrance of them," resumed the old man. "John Foster, who was now established in a handsome house in Portland Place, knew better than to have his fine liveries made by the snob who had provided those of his father. The young ladies married, and one of them died. The family was broken up and dispersed. The fat coachman kept a public-house in the Borough; the fat footman was in an infirmary. I ceased, in short, to hear the smallest mention of the name of Foster; unless when, once a year, I proposed carrying my boy Elias to one of the playhouses, to see the pantomime; when my good woman was sure to observe that no good ever came of going to playhouses;—'For instance,' she would add, 'look at your old favourite, poor Mr. Henry Foster!'—And what was I to answer?

"Well, sir, about five or six years after all I have been telling you, late one summer evening, just at the time that London is so wild with business and pleasure, and it seems as if

poor folks could never work fast enough, or
rich folks be sufficiently idle,—and, having
more than a dozen suits of uniforms, liveries,
and court-dresses to send home for the birthday, (which fell then upon the 4th of June,)
I had just offered extra wages to my men to
work all night, when I heard the voice of a
servant-maid inquiring whether that was the
house of Mr. Jonas Cox, the tailor.

"I answered her myself, and pretty sharply
—for I didn't understand, at that time of
day, any servant of a respectable family being
ignorant of my house of business, fifty years
established on the same spot, sir, as no one
knows better than yourself. But I soon saw
'twas a country lass I had to deal with; and,
in answer to my reprimand, she put into my
hand a bit of paper, on which was written,—
'Mrs. Henry Foster, Crown Inn, Holborn.'

"'Missus says, sir, she would be very glad if
you could make it convenient to call to-night,'
said the girl.

"'Impossible, child,—quite impossible! I
am overwhelmed with business!' cried I,

already out of sorts with the harassing labours of a sultry day, and the prospect of a busy night. 'But tell her I will do my best to be with her before to-morrow evening.'

"And the girl, already terrified by the severity of my first address, had not courage to reply, but hurried out of the shop.

"Next day, I was well nigh forgetting my appointment: but my son, who had heard it made—more, I believe, by way of getting rid of me out of the workshop for an hour, than for any other reason—reminded me of it as evening drew on; and off I started for Holborn.

"A fine summer evening it was, and righ thronged were the streets of the populou part of the town I had to traverse—all th shopkeepers at their open doors to enjoy a breath of air; and the workmen whistling their way homewards for joy, as the birds sing in the country in summer weather. I had got rid of the crossness produced by over-work and fault-finding, by the time I reached Holborn; and was beginning to rejoice at the idea of seeing once more the young couple in whom I had taken so strong an interest. In the interval, all had thriven with *me !*——My business was doubled——my family prosperous. I was in hopes of hearing as much of the Fosters !

" The inn, (they had probably stopped there with the coach on their arrival from Plymouth,) was a narrow-fronted, noisy, gloomy-looking place ; and when I shoved my way into the crowded passage, such a vapour of gas, rum, and tobacco, reeked from the tap, that I wondered how on so close an evening human beings could find pleasure in such an atmosphere. I had some difficulty in making my request to see Mrs. Foster understood by a tawdry-looking, red-faced woman, who was serving at the bar. But as soon as she did understand, a dirty urchin was called from the tap and desired to conduct me up-stairs.

" Up-stairs accordingly we groped, flight after flight, till, on reaching a skylight, through which the remains of a crimson sunset still glimmered, I saw the lad who showed me the way take off his oilskin cap, almost respectfully, as he approached a door, as rickety as all the rest of the premises, which seemed as though the rumble of any heavily laden dray passing the gate would shake into a heap.

" ' The corpse lies there, sir,' said the boy; and so startled was I by the word, that I stood listening to his retreating footsteps down the creaking stairs, instead of opening the door. At length I took courage to tap, —and again and louder, till I found myself bidden to ' come in.'

" As well as I could judge by the glimmering light within, no one was stirring in the chamber but the servant-maid who had come in search of me the preceding night ; who, meeting me at the foot of the curtainless bed, laid her hand upon my arm, and, pointing to it, whispered me to be silent.

" On that bed lay two human forms ; the one, stiff and stretched, with a sheet drawn tight over the rigid limbs ; the other, flung down helplessly beside it, hiding her face in the pillow;——*not* sleeping, for, from time to time, convulsive sobs burst from the bosom of the widow.

" ' Why did you not tell me last night how it was with her?' said I, addressing the girl.

" ' Please to come into the other room, sir, where the little boys are a-bed and asleep,' said she, leading me away, as if apprehensive of telling her sad tale in presence of her poor mistress. And having conducted me into the adjoining closet she called a room, (where, on a flock pallet, lay two little fellows locked in each other's arms,) she told me that her master had expired only the preceding night; that when she came to fetch me, he was alive.

" ' Master had a great wish to see you, sir,' said the girl, whose tears fell bitterly as she told her doleful story. " He was much disappointed, poor gentleman, when he heard that you had spoken harshly, and refused to come.——Master suffered much, sir, in his last moments, but was patienter than a lamb.—— And now, please God, he is in a better place !'——

" I gradually drew from the girl that the Fosters had been a fortnight in town; that poor Mr. Henry had long been declining, suffering from the same inward malady, it was thought, which had carried off his father. He was recommended to go through an operation, and came to London for the purpose, bringing with him a letter of recommendation from the Plymouth Commissioners to one of our eminent army surgeons. But the fatigue and exertion of the journey, accompanied by his family, whom he could not be prevailed upon to leave behind, brought his malady to a crisis. Since his arrival, he had never risen from the bed into which he was moved on quitting the coach; and though in daily hopes that the morrow might effect some improvement in his state, he had gradually sunk. All that remained of my young friend lay under the coarse sheet of an inn-garret in the adjoining room!

" ' What will become of poor missus I know not !' sobbed the girl. ' She has not a friend

in this town. The money which master
brought here is running short. I heard the
undertaker inquiring of the landlord *who* was
to be responsible for the funeral expenses'———

" ' I am afraid your poor mistress was cut
to the soul, my good girl, by my refusing to
come ?' cried I, interrupting her.

" ' Bless you, sir, she has taken no notice
of any mortal thing since, after assisting me
to lay out the body, she threw herself down
beside it. She let the undertakers come and
measure it, as she lay there, without so much
as seeing them.'

" All this was dreadful to think of, sir,"
continued the old tailor, shuddering at the
remembrance; " and, moreover, it happened
at a moment when I had a hard matter to
command time and thought for even my own
business. But this seemed business which
the Almighty had thrown in my way, and it
was not for me to refuse it; so I did my best.
I saw the landlord. I saw the undertaker,
that very night; and the servant-girl being
strange in London, and scarce fit for such a

charge, I sent for the good woman who used
to nurse my own wife, and put her in charge
of children, mother,—ay, and him who was no
more.

" Next day, the young widow was better
able to commune with me; and when she
heard all I had done, would fain have gone
down on her poor knees to thank me. Unknown to me, however, she took strength and
courage to write to her late husband's employers, acquaint them with his untimely end,
and request the means of laying him decently
in the grave.

" Twenty pounds was forwarded by return
of post; a sum that just sufficed to clear the
expenses of the family at the inn, and procure a grave for the departed. I attended as
chief mourner. We buried him in St.
Andrew's churchyard, on a bright June
morning when even the London sky looked
blue and gladsome; and as I stood beside
that humble grave, holding in either hand one
of the poor, sobbing, terrified orphans, whom
he mother insisted should see their father

laid in the ground, I could scarce forbear contrasting that miserable consignment of dust to dust, with the fine pageant proceeding at t'other end of the town, — a mob of embroidered lords a-crowding to court, full of cares and strifes of their own creation, — while in the silent earth at my feet, the wicked ceased from troubling and the weary were at rest!

"The funeral was hurried, at the wish of the landlord,—because in a house of public entertainment the presence of a corpse is injurious. Otherwise, I should have done my best to persuade the widow to attempt an appeal to her rich brother-in-law, John Foster, who could not have refused to bestow upon him a more appropriate interment. But when I hazarded a hint on the subject, she would not hear of any communication with her brother-in-law; nor would she have allowed her husband's remains to be laid in the family vault.

"'You have done me the greatest favour man could do!' said she. 'You have attended

him to his last home.   You have put his boys
into decent mourning, for their father's burial.
These things shall I remember to my dying
day.   But for mercy's sake, no charities from
John Foster!'

"Forced to return to Plymouth to wind
up her affairs, an offer was made her by the
employers of poor Mr. Henry to get her sons
into the government free-school, if she found
it convenient to settle on the spot.   But in
the interim, it occurred to me to apprise John
Foster of the melancholy event without vio-
lating my promise to the widow; and I
accordingly inserted in the newspapers a notice of Mr. Henry's death at the Crown Inn,
Holborn, as 'son to the late John Foster, of
Bedford Row, of the eminent firm of Foster
and Sons, Great St. Helen's.'

"My expectations were verified. Apprehensive that further publicity might be given to
the case, Dives hurried to the scene of his poor
brother's last moments; and learning from
the landlord by whom his funeral had been
attended, condescended to find his way to my
long-forgotten shop.

"I am ashamed to own, sir, that I felt as proud as a prince when I saw the pitiful figure he cut while inquiring into the circumstances of his poor brother's death. I promise you I did not spare him. I could scarcely, indeed, refrain from exclaiming to him, 'Cain, where is thy brother?'

"Not to weary you with details, suffice it that I so mediated between him and the proud widow, that, though for herself she refused all assistance, she suffered a portion of their grandfather's fine fortune to be devoted to the education of the boys. I persuaded her that this was less humiliating than to see them the objects of a public charity.

"Well for them that I did so! For within the year, that heart-broken woman followed her young husband to the grave; and then what would become of the orphans? Moreover, God in his justice had stricken with barrenness the bed of the rich man. There is a Providence above all, sir; and John Foster (like the Scottish usurper in that terrible play which Kemble used to act in my boyhood) had committed crimes in order to acquire a fortune which he had neither chick nor child to inherit !

" 'But what has all this to do,' cried I, 'with the recovery of your debt? Did not the rich man of Harley Street book up with you to the last farthing, after your noble conduct to his brother?'

" He would have doubtless done so, had I put forward a demand. But when the negociations were concluded between him and the widow, she exacted a promise from me that I would never allow him to contribute to the last wants of him who was gone; undertaking to pay me, within the year, with the fruit of her own labours. I gave her my word, and am satisfied she would have kept *hers*, had she not been taken from this world by a summons no man may gainsay. After her death, sir, there was delivered to me a packet in her handwriting, enclosing one which her dying words charged me to remit to her eldest boy, on his attaining twelve years old.

" 'Trust me still, my kind old friend !'

wrote the widow; *trust me in my grave!* My son shall redeem my pledge. Harry will still pay you for the mourning suit he wore at the burial of his father.'

" I thought no more of all this, sir, except to lay by the packet till the appointed time. For I knew the young gentlemen were reared and educated as they ought to be,—that is, as became the worldly position of the uncle by whom they had been adopted. But when the time came appointed by Mrs. Henry's injunctions, I did not shrink from my duty, but betook myself to Harley Street; and with some difficulty obtained access to Master Foster, who was just arrived from Eton for the holidays.

" Such a noble-looking lad ; handsomer even than his poor father at the same age ! When he received me, (in the showy dining-room of his uncle who was absent in the city at his business, and now a widower,) I could scarcel bring to my belief that was the same little fellow to whom I had presented the blue pelisse in Long Acre, ten years before. I thought him a little stiff at first,——perhaps a little proud.——But it was only shyness.——For when I placed his mother's packet in his hand, the colour disappeared from his face, and he trembled like a leaf; and after reading her letter to an end, threw himself in tears into my arms, and even kissed the cheeks of the old tailor, as he would have done those of a relation !"

" A *relation* ?——Say rather of a *benefactor* !" ——cried I, deeply moved.

" And then, such loads of questions as he asked me concerning the miseries of his parents, (not of their *wrongs*——to *them* the mother had wisely refrained from recurring !) and the place where his father was laid,——and ——and——. But the last thing he said vexed me ——It was to implore a renewal of my money engagements with his mother. ' The debt is a sacred one, and mine to discharge,' said the little fellow, with a spirit beyond his years. ' Promise me that you will never accept payment from my uncle ?'

" ' It was not hope of the lucre of gain that

brought me hither, Master Foster,' said I. And then, seeing I was hurt, the poor lad flung his arms round my neck again; and went and fetched his brother Alfred, a more mettlesome but not less handsome boy than himself, to make my acquaintance; telling him I had been the friend of their parents,— ' at one time, indeed,' added Henry, ' their only, *only* friend !'

From that day, I am convinced those two poor young gentlemen must have laid by every guinea of their pocket-money and presents, to accomplish the sacred purpose pointed out by their mother; and for a schoolboy in their condition of life to abjure the indulgences enjoyed by his playmates, is a sacrifice greater than the greatest sacrifices of a man. Right earnest, however, were they in their purpose; for three years afterwards, I received a purse containing sixteen guineas,—in pocket-pieces, new guineas, and a five-pound note, which I afterwards found was a token from Mr. Foster to his elder nephew, on his obtaining high honours in the

school. I wanted to return the money to
them : but they would not hear of it. Only
Master Henry requested my indulgence at
present for the remainder, as they wished to
devote the next portion of their savings to
placing a stone in St. Andrew's churchyard,
over the grave of their father.

"Yesterday, sir——(I am at last bringing
the two ends of my story to meet)——yesterday, sir, as I was tying up my dahlias in my
little garden in Elysium Place, a smart cab
stopped at the door, and a little tiger jump-
ing down, (and, by the way, I never see a
better cut livery since I handled a needle!)
inquires of me, ' whether that was the residence of Mr. Jonas Cox?'——So startled was
I, that I could scarce answer intelligibly ;
for, on going to the gate, I saw there was a
coronet on the harness, and two young gentlemen in the cab.

" ' Wait for me a moment,' said the
youngest of them (a mere lad) to his companion ; and in a moment he had lifted the
garden latch, and (no doubt to the surprise of

the tiger) was shaking me heartily by the
hand, and asking me for a few minutes' conversation in the house.

" ' You don't remember me, I'm sure!'
said he: ' I'm Alfred Foster. You must
have noticed my being gazetted, last month,
into the Guards? I've been to Poland
Street.——I was there a week ago :——but, being
on guard since, and much engaged, could not
find my way here before. A draft upon Cox
and Greenwood, my good friend!' continued
he——placing a paper in my hand. ' But don't
fancy that because this makes money matters
straight between us, Harry or I shall ever
lose sight of our obligations. You would do
us a favour, my dear Mr. Cox, by using this
trifle for our sakes,' said he, placing in my
hands a handsome snuff-box, that bore an in-
scription I scarce could read for the tears in
my eyes! (I would have brought it with me,
sir, this morning, if I had looked forward to
the pleasure of this long chat with you;
though I should be almost ashamed to show
you the flattering words inscribed on't!)

"Before I could say a word in answer to the dear young gentleman, or so much as offer him a receipt in full, (as I doubtless ought,) he was off. Away rolled the cab along the road to Maida Hill; whilst I stood upon the door-steps, staring after it, and looking like an old fool!

"I promise you that Mrs. Cox and I drank the health of young Master Harry and his brother, yesterday, as kindly as I had ever felt inclined to do that of his father! But, thank goodness, 'tis clearing up," cried Cox VI., interrupting himself; "for I've got to call in Poland Street, on my way to the coach-office, to have a peep at the new sheriffs' liveries, which my son has the honour of furnishing. I could tell you a famous story, sir, about those liveries, —— ay, and their master too! But I've tired you and my-self; you shall hear it another time. Good day, sir, good day. I'll bring the snuff-box with me the very first day I'm able to call."

" Much as I wished to see it, however,"
continued my friend, " I did not encourage
the proposal. I had no desire to renew for
the present my 'ACCOUNT WITH A CREDITOR!' "

THE HOT WATER CURE.

Time and tide exercise their influence over the learned professions, as well as over the casualty of Captains.

According to the traditions of the last century, a physician was a well-powdered, elderly gentleman, whose town residence was a well-built London chariot, and whose ensign of office, a gold-headed consulting-cane. After the birthday, it was his custom to order his patients for three or four months into the country, for change of air, while *he* proceeded to his country-seat for the enjoyment of its domestic felicity and sour grapes; such among them as were obstinate enough to be bed-ridden, being assigned for the period of his absence to the well-tied hands of some confidential apothecary.

A physician of the present day, on the

contrary, figures in a natty caoutchouc wig, and highly varnished boots. His town residence stands in a fashionable square, and his bâton of office is the whip of a well-appointed cabriolet. At the close of the season, the fashionable M.D. orders himself to some foreign watering-place——Aix-la-Chapelle, Wiesbaden, Töplitz, or Carlsbad,——the waters of which become indispensable not only to his own health, but to that of all his patients ;——beneficial at once to his own gout,——the plethora of the fat marchioness, —— the dyspepsia of the *roué* duke, and the consumption or hysteria of a whole bevy of fashionable misses !

By this arrangement his professional career becomes as agreeable as profitable, and it will go hard with such a medicus if he do not pick up a Black, White, or Yellow eagle among the German principicules, as a pretext for being beknighted on his return to England.

Once Sir Anything, he has only to get up a quarto on the virtues of Twitchingem, or Switchingem, or some other spa of the Black Forest, affix to his name the initials of his

German order, as well as of the various societies into which he has flummeried himself;
send a well-bound copy to the Emperor of
Russia, to secure a diamond ring in return;
another to Louis Philippe, to fish for a snuff-
box; and a third to Louis of Bavaria, as a
hint for a gold medal; which imperial bene-
factions and regal compliments he duly ad-
vertises, as they successively come to hand,
per paragraph in the morning papers.——And
lo! his fortune is made with the fools of the
fashionable world!

Even such a man is the eminent Sir Jedediah Claversham, &c., &c., &c., &c., &c., &c.,
of Hanover Square; whose portrait may be
admired in the various annual exhibitions,——
in oils, crayons, water-colours,——from miniature to full length,——besides being engraved
in all the print-shops, and stitched in Berlin
work in all the fancy repositories!

Arranged with fitting classification under
glass in his gorgeous drawing-room, lie the
insignia of half-a-dozen orders, a profusion of
gold and silver medals of honour, autograph

letters from crowned heads, diplomas from foreign universities, announcing Sir Jedediah Claversham to be a man of " European reputation." The *beau monde* cannot be ignorant that while his cab is waiting at the door of some dowager in Wilton Crescent, Rome, Dresden, Stockholm, are in agonies of impatience for his answer to their letters. Sir Jedediah is, in short, a modern Boerhaave—a Boerhaave with diamond shirt-studs and white kid-gloves!

The influence which this transformation in the form and pressure of medical capacities may have had on the bills of mortality, is a matter for the consideration of Mr. Wakley, or the discussion of the Statistical Society. Certain it is that our pills have been agreeably gilded by the innovations of the new school; and that a one-and-twenty day fever, prolonged in duration to forty-two, *appears* reduced to a ten days' visitation by the agreeability of the Sir Jedediahs of the day.

By the obsolete order of three-visits-and-three-draughts-a-day-apothecaries, a malady

was rendered a calamity indeed; whereas the
travelled Esculapii execute for the sick and
ailing world all that Howell and James perform for the fashionable; by the assiduous
importation of the last new novelties and spring
fashions of the continent. While the jog-trot
men of routine still extant in the quizzical
old College of Physicians, or their snail-shells
in Baker Street or Bloomsbury, adhere to
rhubarb, senna, and the Pharmacopeia Lon-
donensis or Edinensis, the Sir Jedediahs come
back from the continent at the expiration of
every cholera-season, bringing with them, by
the Antwerp steamer, some monstrous nos-
trum or patent device, such as curing consumption by the application of bear's-grease
to the soles of the feet, or removing tubercles
from the lungs by baths of ox-tail soup!—
One year, homœpathy is their stalking-horse;
—the next, brandy and salt;—the third, the
cold water cure!

The importation of Sir Jedediah last season,
however, still remains an anonymous mystery
—a cure without a name!—Homœpathy has

long been vulgarized by the press; and Vincent Preissnitz became a by-word the moment his book of revelations was seen in print; warned by which experience, Sir Jedediah chose to be as mute as a mummy concerning a new system of medical treatment, to which he is reported to have become a convert at the baths of Mehadia, in Hungary, in consultation with the body-physician of Georgewitsch Czerny, Prince of Servia, called in with him to attend the hysterical waiting-maid of an English dowager of fashion; by whom, rumours of the wondrous works of her united doctors were circulated on her return, throughout half the country-houses of Great Britain.

In the course of the spring, accordingly, Sir Jedediah began to foresee the necessity for doubling the returns of his profits to the income-tax commissioners. Patients sprang under his feet like mushrooms? Still, he uttered not a word. When applied to by a dozen applicants for a programme of his performances,—when requested by letters from

Ireland or the Land's End, to state whether his mode of practice were founded on electropathy, or hydropathy, or any other newly-invented pathy,—he contented himself with replying that he possessed no exclusive mode of practice; and that all he demanded was "the power of communicating with his patient in person and alone."

The immediate consequence of this regulation was the establishment of two new hotels, and the letting of all the old lodging-houses in the vicinity of Hanover Square; at the various doors of which, the cab of the fashionable physician is still seen in daily waiting, in doses of half an hour at a time. Already, wonders are related of the healing influence of these visits. Four countesses dying of nervous fever,—three honourable misses subject to spasms,—the young Viscount Benledi, who inherits seventy thousand a year and a liver complaint,—to say nothing of an eminent ex-member of parliament, given over in an atrophy,—have been successively redeemed from the brink of the grave by the

miraculous spells of Sir Jedediah Claversham,
&c., &c., &c. !!

I plead guilty to a weakness for new inventions. Through life, I have been a martyr
to patents, and my lumber-room is encumbered
with lamps " on an entirely novel principle,"
which could never be made to burn, and locks
of scientific mechanism, which could never be
kept shut. Having the misfortune to enjoy
perfect health, I had, however, no pretext for
searching into the mysteries of the Prince of
Servia's body physician. But I have the good
fortune to possess an intimate friend in a
highly infirm state of nerves, a lady of fashion
and fortune, for whose recovery, having nothing to hope from her will, I am deeply interested,—some months ago I persuaded *her*
to consult Sir Jedediah.

" I am too ill and nervous to see strangers,"
was her reply, drawing her cachemere shawl
more closely round her stooping shoulders.

" But a physician is never a *stranger*,"—
said I, "and Sir Jedediah will *cure* you of
being weak and nervous."

"No, no! He will do as all the others have done,—advise air, exercise, exertion;—exertion to *me*, who have scarcely strength to turn on my sofa!—These doctors come here, themselves in robust health, from visiting the wife of some country squire; and fancy that a person of *my* susceptibility is to be treated in the same manner!—Physician is but another name for savage."

"Sir Jedediah is the most amiable person on the face of the earth," cried I. "At Vienna he is cited as more courteous than the ambasdor. He has figured at all the courts in Europe. At Rome, he used to drink tea with the Pope; and the Hetman of the Cossacks offered him five millions of rubles a year and the hand of his niece, to become his household physician!"

"Well, well! I will try to think about it," said Lady Anne. "My nerves are so wretchedly shattered that even the mention of a new name makes me tremble from head to foot."

Nerves, indeed!—A solitary prisoner, month after month, in a boudoir fifteen feet square, with the thermometer at 80°, and the atmosphere charged with the emanations of cape jessamines, tuberoses, and *sachets* of *vitivert* and *maréchale*, living on a diet of green tea, French novels, and *échaudés* !——One of Meux's dray-horses could not have stood it a week! ——I was forced, however, to leave poor dear Lady Anne to the enjoyment of her vagaries; for soon afterwards, I crossed the channel for a ramble through Normandy.

On my return to town, finding still a remnant left of the season, I sauntered into Hyde Park, where, in the fervours of July, the fashionable world concentrates itself, as is its custom of an afternoon, from six to eight o'clock, in open carriages, stationary beside the cool waters of the Serpentine; surrounded by equestrians, male and female, engaged in the smallest of small-talk with the fair loungers of the britzkas and barouches.

To my utter surprise, the first carriage that met my view was that of the charming Lady Anne; confronting the keen air of the dog-days with only half-a-dozen India shawls and

boas for her protection !—I approached with
my congratulations on this auspicious conva-
lescence.

" It is all Sir Jedediah's doing," said she,
cordially accepting my shake of the hand.
" Sir Jedediah is the cleverest creature in the
world !"

" You have seen him, then, at last ?"

" Seen him ?—I would not pass a day *without* seeing him, for the universe !—My life is
in his hands !"—

" And may I inquire," said I, " by what
charm he has wrought this last and greatest
of miracles ?"—

" I cannot tell you if I would," replied her
ladyship ; " though as my first adviser in the
business you are in every way entitled to my
confidence !   Between ourselves, Sir Jedediah
calls it THE HOT WATER CURE; why, I am
sure, I cannot conjecture ; for he expressly
interdicts the use of the warm bath.   However, come to my house to tea this evening,
and I will explain the whole affair."

A few months before and I would sooner

have gone to drink caudle with some Welsh
curate's prolific consort than tea with my fair
cousin.   But the prospect of the development
of the grand mystery of ———pathy tempted
me sorely.——At nine o'clock, therefore, I entered the well-known boudoir in Chesterfield
Street.

Nothing was altered. The same subdued
light——the same hermetically-closed windows
——the same overpowering scent of heliotropes
and orange-blossom——the same *bonbonnières*
scattered about.——Everything I had been accustomed to notice in her delicate retreat was
still there; with the exception of the last
H. B., and the latest novel of Balzac.

" You may remember," said Lady Anne in
a cheerful voice, inviting me to take my place
beside her, as soon as we had swallowed two
tiny cups of coffee, yellow and transparent as
a Cairn-Gorm pebble, " how utterly lost I
was when you quitted London. Chambers
had ordered me to Nice,——Holland insisted
on my wintering at Malta. So reduced
was I, that three wafers and half an ice

a day were almost too much for my diges-
tion ; while my spirits were in such a flutter-
ing state that I was obliged to order poor
Flora into Mademoiselle's room, not being
able to bear the excitement of her company.
In short, my dear, I felt my end to be approaching.——I had signed my will, and every
now and then added a codicil——instructions
for which, to my men of business, served only
to increase my depression ; when, at your desire, I sent, as a last resource, to Sir Jedediah.
Aware that he only came to see me die by
inches, I could have no objection to comply
with your wishes, and *let* him see me die !"

Assuming a becoming face of sympathy, I
patted the head of poor Flora, now restored
to her former post of honour beside her lady.

" Never shall I forget," resumed Lady Anne,
" the evening on which that inestimable man
paid me his first visit !——The morning had
been rainy, with that small, still, spring rain,
so far from conveying the excitement of a
summer shower. All day, one had known
that it would rain all day :——that there would

be no intermission, and consequently no droppers-in,——no chat,——no news,——no anything! By degrees, as the dusk grew on, I felt absolutely exterminated. The long evening of a solitary invalid was before me ;——too close for a fire,——too damp for an open window ;——even the hissing of the tea-urn, after sinking to a low humming murmur, subsided into silence. As you are well aware, Chesterfield Street is no thoroughfare, and my boudoir overlooks the quiet gardens of Chesterfield House. All, all, therefore, was still as death, — still as the family vault into which I felt myself to be gradually sinking. Amid the general gloom, I could hear the faint ticking of the Bréguet watch that lies on yonder console. When lo ! the door was quietly opened, and without fuss or announcement, a gentlemanly, middle-aged man, entered and took a seat,——near me, but not commanding a view of my face ; so that my agitation at his unexpected appearance was unobserved.

"I have to apologize," said Sir Jedediah, "for not attending to your ladyship's application by an earlier visit. (Give me leave to feel your pulse?) An engagement of a very peculiar nature rendered it impossible for me so much as to reply to your ladyship's note. (May I request to see your tongue?) I consoled myself with the earnest hope of being able to wait upon your ladyship this evening. The weather, I am happy to say, has cleared up,—the night is delicious,—and so soft a temperature that, with your ladyship's permission, I will slightly open the opposite window."

"Open the window?" faltered I, too weak, however, for opposition. "I have not exposed myself to the night-air, even in July, these three years past."

"I have opened it only wide enough to admit the interposition of a sheet of *very* thin Bath post," replied Sir Jedediah, resuming his place, while a gentle air gradually expanded in the apartment, not altogether unrefreshing. "We will close it in less than five minutes, by my chronometer. As I said before, I would fain have waited upon your ladyship last night, but for a singular adventure, which has, I fear, been a source of disappointment to several of my expectant patients. But the circumstances were *so* peculiar,—so VERY peculiar,—I may say, so unprecedented—"

A tremor seemed to invade his voice as he spoke, and involuntarily I fixed my inquiring eyes upon his face. There is something in the aspect of a strong man subdued to weakness by struggles of powerful emotion, peculiarly exciting.

"I had just risen from dinner yesterday evening, and was about to enter my study for the purpose of answering your ladyship's note," resumed Sir Jedediah, in answer to my mute interrogation, "when I was startled by a loud knock at my door; and my servant entering, inquired whether I would be at home to a gentleman who had called in his cabriolet. I inquired his name. The gentleman had expressly declared such announcement to be of no consequence, as he was not one of my habitual patients. Not caring to be interrupted in my purpose of replying to

your ladyship, I sent word that I was particularly engaged, and must decline the honour
of his visit. The gentleman, it seems, persisted; for a few minutes afterwards, my
confidential servant returned, with the sort of
deprecating air he assumes whenever his feelings have been especially appealed to by persons desiring to consult me; and whispered
that, 'if not particularly inconvenient, the
stranger was *most anxious* for the honour of
an interview.'

"Conceiving that a quarter of an hour was
the utmost sacrifice of time he required of
me, I rashly complied; and immediately
afterwards a light step hastened along the
hall, and a young man, personally unknown
to me, glided into the room. Tall, graceful,
strikingly handsome, his fine open countenance evinced tokens of considerable emotion
as he offered a thousand incoherent apologies
for his unauthorized intrusion at such an
hour.

"'If the case admitted of the least delay,'
said he, directing his large gray eyes plead-

ingly towards mine, ' I had not been thus
ungraciously persevering. But alas ! not a
moment is to be lost ! I have to entreat you
will accompany me a mile or two out of town
to visit a patient in the most urgent need of
your assistance.' "

" And you had no idea *who* was the person
thus addressing you ?" said I (for I could not
help surmising that I was better informed on
the subject than Sir Jedediah).

"Not the slightest ! —— The stranger was
about five feet eleven, with a high forehead
and arched eyebrows,——a Roman nose, delicately chiselled, and the handsomest mouth I
ever remember to have seen."

" It *must* have been Lord Charles L—— !"
was my secret reflection, but I uttered not a
syllable, to indicate any peculiar interest in
the matter.

" I assured my visitor," resumed Sir Jedediah, " that it was totally out of my power to
comply with his request ; that I had letters
to write—visits to pay ; ——in short, the thing
was impossible. Still he pleaded so urgently

the importance of the case, that it was difficult to persist in denial.

" ' I ask only the sacrifice of an hour,' said
he, with the most feeling earnestness, ' an
hour, vital to the existence of a fellow-crea-
ture, — to the happiness of many !—*Can* you
have the inhumanity to refuse ?' "

" I am convinced that you had *not !*" interrupted I, becoming gradually interested in his
narrative.

" Your ladyship has judged me rightly !
Laying aside my writing materials, I rang for
my hat and gloves, and proposed ordering my
carriage.

" ' No, no, doctor,' replied the young man ;
' it is almost as essential that you should be
unaccompanied by servants in this visit, as
that you should come at all.   *My* cab is at
the door.——My horse is notoriously the fastest
stepper in London.' "

" It *must* have been Lord Charles," thought
I, " whose bay is the most noted cab-horse
about town."

" In short, madam, he persuaded me to

jump into his cabriolet; and, though I flatter
myself my own horse is citable for speed, I
was almost startled by the pace at which I
soon found myself proceeding down the Bays-
water Road. We had soon passed Hyde
Park Terrace, —— Kensington Gravel-pits,——
Notting Hill——till, when we finally attained
the park palings of Holland House, I ventured
to inquire whether we had not *almost* attained
our destination. Even at the rate we were
proceeding, I could not but be aware, as we
approached Acton, that allowing only twenty
minutes for my professional visit, on my return the hour specified must be far exceeded.

" 'We have still somewhat more than a
mile before us,' said my companion, breaking
silence in a husky voice. 'My horse knows
the road, doctor, as *you* know your own
hearthrug.'

" Touching the noble animal slightly on the
flank as he spoke, it started off anew; and
though I could only discover by the aroma or
effluvia of the atmosphere that we were skirt-
ing alternately clover-fields, brick-fields, and

hay-fields, we kept the winding road as stea-
dily as though it were the well-worn ring of
Hyde Park.

" ' The cross-road, though the nearest cut
from Marylebone to Kingston, is wholly un-
frequented at night,' observed my companion. ' One never meets so much as a foot-
passenger.'

" ' Nor is there a house for half a mile
round,—which is singular enough so near the
metropolis,'—replied I, peeping out through
the darkness of the night, in hopes of discovering *some* habitation across the dreary pastures.

" ' Not one!' resumed he, in an empha-
tic tone ; and in spite of myself, and the
gentlemanly deportment I had remarked in
my companion, I could not forbear wishing
that, when consenting to become the companion of a total stranger in such an expedition,
I had left my pocket-book and gold repeater
behind."

" You surely did not mistake him for a
highwayman ?" escaped my lips.

" I knew not what to infer from his taci-
turnity, and a certain mysterious reserve
whenever I ventured to renew my inquiries
concerning the unknown patient to whom we
were hurrying.   With growing anxiety did I
watch, by the reflected light of the lamps, the
hedges go by, at the end of which I knew we
must approach the populous confines of Chis-
wick.   At length the welcome fragrance of
gardens,——the happy, domestic flower-border
scent of stocks and mignonette, apprized me
that human habitations were at hand.——We
emerged into the Great Western Road, and
my momentary mistrust was instantly dissi-
pated ! Life,——noise,——lamp-posts,——lights,——
turnpikes,——omnibuses,——renewing the ordinary occupations of life,——seemed to restore
my confidence in my companion.

" ' We are now more than five miles distant
from Hyde Park Corner ! ' cried I, finding
myself thus deceived as to time.

" ' And the worst of it is,' was his cool reply, as he turned his head towards town,
' that we must, in the first instance, retrace

our steps. The first turn to Hammersmith will bring us into the Fulham Road.'

" Into the Fulham Road he accordingly soon announced himself to have turned. But so dark was the night, that I was utterly unable to discover my whereabout. All I could determine was, that we were threading our way through market-gardens, dotted with dwarf fruit-trees, and savouring powerfully of onion-beds and melon-grounds.

" 'We are on the direct road to our place of destination!' was his mysterious reply; a reply so mysterious, that my previous anxieties were on the eve of returning; and I took it into my head that one or two turns and doublings attempted by my driver were solely intended to deceive me as to our direction.

" 'It is now an hour since we left my house,' said I, striking my repeater; when, by the increased freshness of the atmosphere, we seemed to be approaching the river. 'The time is already exceeded which you demanded of me; and I must insist upon knowing either your own name or that of the patient to whom you are conducting me.'

"‘In five minutes, your very natural inquiry will be answered by the individual in question,’ replied he, wholly undisturbed by my abrupt apostrophe. ‘We are now approaching the house.’

. "The lane we were threading was narrow and tedious; but I soon perceived that on the side nearest, as I supposed to the river, the hitherto straggling hedge was replaced by a paling, overtopped by a shrubbery. The fragrance of a choice flower-garden was perceptible in the air. In another moment, we paused beside a row of lofty trees, which, though bordering an opposite field, threw their shade over both paling and shrubbery, and formed a sort of natural portico to a rustic gateway. My companion, giving the reins into my hand, now alighted, and rang a bell, which, in the silence of that secluded place, sounded so loud and shrill, that I fancied the signal must be audible at half a mile distance, instead of requiring to be repeated again and again, ere servants appeared at the gate.   One of them instantly advanced to the horse's head : I leapt from the cabriolet.

" I can scarcely say by what concatenation of ideas, but, as I traversed the gravel-walk of what appeared to be a delightful cottage residence or rustic villa, there occurred to my mind the vulgar tragedy of Weare, and Gill's Hill Lane, with which, thanks to newspapers and melodramas, all London was painfully familiarized some twenty years ago.

" Ashamed, however, of these misgivings, I silently followed my companion towards what, by the light of the reflector carried by an aged servant out of livery who preceded us, appeared to be a rustic wall formed of fragments of rough-hewn stone, piled after the fashion of rock-work, and partially covered with creeping and trailing plants.   In the centre was a simple garden doorway, on either side of which were niches — the one containing a fine marble statue of a saint in adoration—the other of a dancing Faun.   I had leisure to note these particulars while the servant applied a patent key to an interstice of the wall, close beside which, a door, apparently of weighty bronze, revolved slowly on its hinges, and displayed within (in lieu of the open garden I had expected) the square, well-lighted vestibule of a comfortable mansion! The floor, of white marble, was traversed by a single breadth of scarlet cloth, towards an inner-door of polished mahogany, leading to a smaller octangular vestibule, from which four doors appeared to open into as many apartments; the intersecting angles having niches containing simple canephoræ of white marble for the support of lamps. As we entered this second vestibule (the floor of which was muffled by a thick Turkey carpet), I overheard the aged servant whisper to my young companion, ' I am charged to conduct the gentlemen into the armoury.'

" 'Good!' was the succinct reply; and the old man having thrown open a door to the left, I found myself in a small but admirably proportioned chamber. The walls and floor were of highly polished Silesian granite; the latter being covered in the centre with a circular Indian mat, surrounded by low seats of carved ebony, with cushions of curiously-embossed velvet; while the walls were garnished on all sides with trophies of rich armour, symmetrically disposed. Stands of assorted arms filled up the angles of the chamber; and on casting my eyes inquiringly around, I perceived, by the imperfect light of a single lamp standing on the granite chimneypiece (under which smouldered a few dying brands, lighted probably on rainy days even in summer, to secure the armour from rust), that the collection was of rare beauty and elegance, comprising princely specimens of Italian plating, — of Damascus work, — of chain-mail, — of Toledo steel, — the murky kreese of the Malayan warriors — the jewelled claymore of the Highland chief.

" 'An antiquary might here find ample room for his researches!' said I, intending to address the young man by whom I had been accompanied from town. But on turning round, astonished by his silence, I found that he had disappeared.

" ' I seem to have fallen among a strange set of people !' was my secret reflection, as I fixed my eyes on a complete suit of Milan steel, richly incrusted with gold, of the fourteenth century—the scaled gauntlets of which had done honour to the workshop of a Bond Street goldsmith ! And lo ! as I stood absorbed in contemplation, the niche or panel in which the suit was suspended appeared suddenly to recede, and I found that the figure served only to mask a doorway into an adjoining apartment, which now lay open before me.

" If my glance at the elaborate richness of the armoury, with its wealth of daggers, pistols, shields, and cuirasses, had impressed me with the conviction that the owner was not only a man, but a man of noble fortune, as well as warlike tendencies and pursuits, the room I *now* entered inspired me with a far different conviction ! At all events, the wealthy invalid had decidedly a female companion in his luxurious solitude ;—

A hermit with an angel for his guest !

" It was a music-room : the walls, consisting of that dazzling white stucco which
Russia has so successfully imported into Europe from the East, were delicately painted in
compartments after the Etruscan fashion, with
a selection of the most exquisite designs discovered at Herculaneum, each bearing classi-
cal reference to the arts of harmony.   The
floor was formed of highly-polished engrained
woods to correspond ; so that no extrinsic
obstacle intervened to impede the sound of
the instrument.   In the centre of the room,
in a moveable orchestra furnished with seats
and desks, stood a grand pianoforte, in a
simple rosewood case, a harp, and a variety
of stringed and wind instruments, in their
cases.

" One side of the room was furnished with
a library of music-books, richly bound, bearing on their backs the names of the greatest
composers of all countries—such as Matthew
Locke, Purcell, Palestrina, Gluck, and Beet-
hoven ; and in this, as in the adjoining chamber, no windows disturbed the harmony of the

architecture.   The light was exclusively admitted from above, through the domed ceiling ;
the villa being evidently constructed after the
single-storied architecture of the ancients.

"But I am wearing your ladyship with all
these details," cried Sir Jedediah, suddenly
interrupting himself.

"On the contrary," cried I, "I am inexpressibly interested by your narrative.   I
fancied myself acquainted with all the villas
of note in the neighbourhood of town——Chis-
wick, Rose-bank, Sion ;——but I would give
worlds to visit anything so new and original
as the place you describe."

"I confess I was as much struck by the
reality as your ladyship's more impressible sen-
sibilities appear to be by my crude and meagre
description !   I stood transfixed, lost in sur-
mises concerning the luxurious Sybarite by
whose imagination this rare retreat had been
called into existence.   If the personal charms
of the fair creature, the presiding genius of
such a music-room, were in any degree corre-
spondent with its beauty and elegance, he

was indeed to be envied! But *who* could he be?——Your ladyship has named the most opulent of our aristocratic enchanters?——I could myself point out the suburban villas of almost every man of note or notoriety. What mysterious epicurean was this?

"My mind was bewildered by conjectures! At the extremity of the music-room, was a recess; the nature and extent of which was concealed by muslin draperies. But ere I had been many minutes in the room, these curtains being gently withdrawn by cords arranged within, discovered a table covered with wines and liqueurs, cakes, and fruit, served in a magnificent style. It was neither quite a woman's refection, nor altogether a man's. For the former, tea was wanting; for the latter, still more substantial diet. Untempted, however, by the elegance with which the little banquet was set out, I pursued my examination of the fresco paintings around me; which, from the transparent whiteness of the stucco, had the effect of being painted on porcelain. So much indeed was I engrossed by the examination of their exquisite execution, that I heeded not the progress of time, till reminded of the unfair encroachment on my own, by an alabaster timepiece placed on an adjoining bracket; which, after the chiming of the hour, struck up one of Auber's brilliant boleros, as if to cheer the progress of the night.

" I now looked round the room for a bell to summon back the aged servant, and express my indignation at being paraded like a child through the curiosities of a showhouse, on pretence that my professional services were seriously required. Resolved to be no longer trifled with, I made up my mind to order the cabriolet, and drive myself back to town, in case the patient, to whom I had been assured my services were indispensable, should be still unprepared to receive me, or my former companion to escort my return.

Bell, however, there was none. The exquisite and almost poetical distribution of the house, was not to be polluted by anything so matter-of-fact as a bell-pull. Mechanically, therefore, I clapped my hands, as I have seen

practised in the East, though rather as a relief
to my impatience than from any expectation
of finding my signal obeyed. To my great
surprise, the gray-headed servant instantly
made his appearance.

"No need to avow my irritability, or signify my impatience. Without a word spoken,
the old man made me a sign to follow him ; and
passing through the recess, from which meanwhile the table had silently disappeared (probably by the mechanical process used at the
old palace of Choisy, or that of the Hermitage
at St. Petersburg), I entered a third chamber, more striking, if possible, than the two
former ones:——half-saloon, half-library, having
on a sofa-table a single silver branch, the candles of which were concealed under a cupola
of green Bohemian glass. Impossible to be
more pleasingly subdued than the light emitted ! The hangings of the room were of a
straggling, dark-patterned, Indian chintz——
the ground being so white and so highly-
glazed as to assume the appearance of marble.
The furniture, covered with the same material,

was composed of unpolished rosewood. On the sofa-table, supporting the light, lay a carpet woven of Indian reeds; and opposite the table, were folding-doors opening through a small conservatory, trellised with the most curious floriferous exotics, to the lawn beyond, the fragrant freshness of which penetrated deliciously into the apartment."

"Instinctively, I drew a deep breath at this picture of luxurious enjoyment."

"Is the window too much for your ladyship?" cried Sir Jedediah, rising and bringing back the sheet of Bath post, in token of having closed it in deference to the susceptibility of my chest.

"By no means!" I breathlessly exclaimed, as he returned from the window. "But no matter," cried I, impatiently, lest he should lose time in replacing it. "I entreat of you, continue your narrative. Was this charming morning-room also unoccupied?"

"At first, I thought it deserted like the rest; but a low murmuring sound gradually attracted my attention to a chaise-longue placed to the right of the table near the door; and no sooner had my eyes accommodated themselves to the glimmering light of the place, than I perceived an emaciated figure, in a loose wrapper, extended thereupon."

"*A woman?*" cried I, half rising from my own recumbent posture, inexpressibly interested.

" No, madam; the form was that of a man; —his head, white with age (if I might judge by the few hairs straggling around his temples), was covered by a black silk skull-cap, increasing the solemnity of his appearance. The lineaments of his finely-formed face were of striking beauty; though painfully attenuated by age or indisposition. Concluding him to be asleep, for he stirred neither hand nor foot, I stole towards the sofa, with the view of feeling his pulse, and ascertaining if possible the nature of his temperament and its irregularities, while thus absorbed in repose.

" Scarcely, however, had I touched the sleeve of his robe, when he started up with the activity of a man twenty years of age, and motioned me to draw towards the sofa one of the stools with which the chamber was furnished. Objecting to a seat so incommodious, I looked round for an arm-chair. There was but one in the room——an American rocking-chair, of patent iron, painted to imitate bamboo, which tempted me as little as the *plians* to which I was now fain to have recourse.

"'Do you speak French, sir?' inquired the old gentleman, in a low, melodious voice, but with a peculiarly distinct enunciation; and on my answering in the affirmative, he renewed his conversation in that language.

"'Are you, pray, one of those doctors,' was his abrupt inquiry, 'who fancy the emanations of stramonium fatal as those of the upas?'

"An incoherent query, which I should have attributed to aberration of intellect, had he not pointed to a fine *Dhatura Arborea* in full bloom, planted in the adjoining conservatory.

" ' If you are afraid of it,' said he, ' the folding-doors shall be closed in a second.'

" ' Not on my account, sir,' was my reply. ' I have certainly been led to believe the emissions of the plant of a nature highly injurious to human life. But *your* position opposes a direct contradiction to the prejudice. You would not of course be lying within scope of the vapour, had not your previous experience ascertained it to be innocuous.'

" ' I sometimes fancy poisons have less ascendency over *my* constitution than those of other men,' replied the old gentleman, waving his head, and assuming a mournful tone. ' However, you have nothing to fear from yonder beautiful Dhatura. I have seen a child sleep unharmed under its branches.'

" Having no time to waste in discussions of natural history, I now took occasion to inquire of my companion the nature of his ailments.

" ' Of *my* ailments ?' cried he, greatly surprised.

" 'It is at your command, sir, I conclude, that I am summoned hither?' said I, coldly.

" 'By my command—certainly. But do *I* look like an ailing man? Am *I* a subject for the charlatanry of mountebanks,—for the experiments of a physician?'

" 'Your advanced age, sir,' I was beginning —but the mercurial old man started to his feet to interrupt me.

" 'Age?' cried he, — 'age is a chimera! The Pyramids are what is called old; but any row of houses run up last week on Brixton Hill, is a thousand times more decrepit! I am a boy, sir!—I never experienced an ailment in my life, or consulted a leech in this or any other country.'

" 'In that case, sir,' said I, rising to take leave of one at whose strangeness I was beginning to stand almost in awe, 'I have no business here. Suffer me, therefore, to take my leave.'

" 'You are tolerably hasty for one whose business it is to bear with the peculiarities and regulate the irregularities of mankind,'

retorted he, with a cynical smile. 'If I sent
for you hither, Sir Jedediah, it was neither
for the purpose of refreshing your lungs (jaded
by the enervating vapours of sick-rooms), by
a country night-ride, nor for the ostentation
of introducing a stranger into my Tusculum
(though, by the way, you might return as you
came, little the worse for having been com-
pelled to either enjoyment) — No, no, sir!
Your professional attendance here has a spe-
cific object, and will be suitably remunerated.'

" 'My impatience, sir, is less interested
than you seem to suppose,' cried I, with indignation. 'I am desirous of coming to the
point, chiefly because my presence is required
elsewhere.'

" 'Be a physician where he may, his presence is probably required elsewhere,' retorted the eccentric old man. 'Such is the
exigence of the profession. As to disinterest-
edness—but for the temptation of a fee—a
man must be indeed filthily minded to become
a physician,—a mere groper into the bodily
infirmities of his fellow-creatures. By all the

mummies of the Pharaohs! I would fain think better of the understanding of my learned leech, than suppose him indifferent to the amount of his guerdon.'

"So saying, he took from under the pillow of his chaise-longue a purse containing, apparently, about a hundred pieces of gold, and almost flung it into my lap.

"'A very moderate portion of this will satisfy my claims, when you have done me the honour to consult me,' said I, laying it coldly on the table.

"'How know you that?' cried the old gentleman. 'What can you surmise of the nature of the service required of you, for which I thus tender pre-payment?'

"'What, indeed!—or how can *you*, sir, determine whether it may suit me to accept either the office or the charge?'

"'A physician is servant of the public,' said the old cynic, scornfully.

"'But not its slave! I, at least, being independent in circumstances, am not to be hired, like a hackney-coach, by the first

comer.   In proof of which, sir, I have the
honour to wish you a good night.   I am not
used to be thus peremptorily dealt with.'

" The old man shrugged his shoulders, im-
plying that he thought me a blockhead ; and
having pushed the heavy purse towards him,
I prepared for instant departure.

" ' Not quite so fast, doctor,' cried he ; ' I
do not like you the less for this little outburst
of spirit.   You are just the man described to
me,—a pepper-pot, but a gentleman.   Some
day or other, we shall perhaps be better acquainted ; and exercise mutual forbearance
towards each other's oddities.—Seat yourself,
and listen.'

" A command to ' seat oneself and listen '
usually prognosticates a long story.   My time
being sadly bespoken, I was forced to be
chary of it, and my vexation being, I suppose,
depicted in my countenance, the old gentleman exclaimed, with a dry, short laugh,—

" ' Ha ! ha !   You are afraid I should keep
you maundering on till midnight, eh ?   Don't
be alarmed, as some fellow or other said about

the parson and his lengthy sermon ;——the man
who can't explain his meaning in half an hour,
doesn't understand his business.   Twenty minutes, sir, and you are free !—— Moreover,
throughout your intercourse with me, your
time will be exactly calculated and honour-
ably remunerated. —— And now to business.
What may be your opinion, pray, of the
young fellow who brought you hither to-
night ?'

    " ' As we have not been three hours ac-
quainted, and our acquaintance is of the
slightest kind,' I was beginning——

    " ' Pho ! pho ! pho !' interrupted the strange
old man ; ' no one is ever ten minutes alone
with another, without imbibing decided impressions concerning him,——like or dislike,——
confidence or mistrust.   Out with your notions !——What did you think of him ?'——

    " As he spoke, he rolled the light sofa
nearer to the table, and peered into my eyes.

    " ' That he appeared a very gentlemanly
young man,' said I.

    " ' Gentlemanly ?——Ha ! ha !——The merit of

his tailor, hatter, hosier ! Say more, or say
nothing !—— Answer me at once, doctor !——
Would you not intrust yourself blindly to his
hands ?——Are you not satisfied, from a certain
air of high blood and breeding in his person
and manners, that you have only honourable
entertainment to expect at his hands ?'

" ' I have already, sir, afforded some proof
of confidence in your young friend,' said I ;
' nor is it as yet diminished by my experience.'

" ' Ha ! ha !——stiff and straightforward as a
crocodile !' cried the old man. ' But you are
wasting the time which, as you observed, just
now, is not your own. In a word, the patient
concerning whom I am interested to procure
your opinion, abides not in this house ; nor do
I choose you to know to *what* house you are
conducted for the purpose of an interview.——
Will you, therefore, submit to be blindfolded,
to accompany the same gentleman in the same
cab, half an hour's distance from this spot ?'

" ' Certainly not !' said I. ' Though free
from apprehension of personal ill-usage, I respect myself too much to act in concert with

those who evince a total want of confidence in my discretion.'

" ' I have as much confidence in your discretion as in any other person's,' replied my singular host. ' But the best of us are babblers and boasters. It is not, however, so much what you will whisper to-morrow at your club of which I stand in fear, as the influence of name and position in your verdict upon the patient; — an eminent person,—a person whose antecedents are so well known to yourself and all the world, that your opinion *must* be prejudiced. You would ground your judgment upon circumstances, not upon observation. — Whereas, I am desirous of a fresh, free, and unshackled decision on a case that has interested hundreds of your brethren in this and other countries.'

" Once more, it occurred to me that I was conversing with a man of disturbed intellects; and with his former perspicuity he interpreted the look of uneasiness contracting my brows.

" ' No, doctor, I am not mad !—saner perhaps than yourself in this matter.'

" 'My determination, sir, has never wavered,' said I. 'As a physician of regular practice, I have no occasion to digress into adventures and mummeries, to increase my list of patients. Such tricks as blindfolding, or masking, have their fitting place in the pages of a second-rate novel, or the scenes of some vulgar melodrama; but are out of my line of business. Permit me, therefore, to ring for the carriage that brought me hither.'

" 'You *refuse?*——refuse, with a hundred golden reasons for compliance glittering before you?' said the old gentleman, withdrawing his chin from his bony hands, and clenching them with rage.

" 'I refuse!'

" 'But have you the *right* to refuse?' persisted he. "When once a man, by the combined force of genius, study, and experience, attains *your* eminence in the profession, has he a right to withhold his aid from an unfortunate being, struggling against a cruel malady and the blunders of the faculty, whom his advice may restore to an afflicted family?'

" I was not to be deluded by the flatteries thus plausibly applied.

" ' Let me see my patient, sir, by fair means, in the ordinary way,' cried I, ' and my utmost exertions will evince the sincerity of my professional zeal.'

" Instead of replying, the old man clapped his hands so eagerly, that I concluded my terms were about to be complied with. The venerable servant instantly reappeared.

" ' Conduct this gentleman to the stables,' said he ; ' the chariot will instantly convey him as speedily as possible back to town.—Do me the justice to accept this remuneration for your visit,' concluded he, forcing five guineas into my hand. ' My young friend cannot drive you home again, as he must instantly seek the services of some more accommodating medical attendant.'—

" Some signal may have passed at the same time between the master and his attendant for I was, I admit, so nettled at his imperious mode of dismissing me, that I followed the domestic rapidly out of the room, with the expectation of being recalled ere I reached the carriage.

" As I traversed the vestibule, I determined to demand an interview with the young man who had escorted me down. But scarcely had I stepped upon the gravel of the entrance-drive, when, turning to signify my wishes to my companion, I found myself alone. The house-door had suddenly closed upon me, and all was darkness.

" It was not difficult to retrace the few steps I had advanced from the door, but, having regained it, what did I obtain? There was neither bell nor knocker. All that met my hands amid the darkness of the night was the cold bronze of the knob-nailed portal; to make myself heard through which, was as if to knock at the tomb of the Capulets.

" Beyond, on either side, extended only the rugged fragments of rock-work, forming the wall of this mysterious habitation; along which I crept, first to the right, then to the left, till they became unapproachable behind the thorny holly-branches of the shrubbery.——

Not a window, not a loophole,—not a means of ingress in any direction.—The only objects I encountered in my researches were the clammy, bloated leaves of the cacti and other trailing plants; which, moistened with dew, revolted the touch like the slimy skin of some noisome, crawling reptile.——

"Having wasted more than an hour in infructuous attempts to re-enter the house, make myself heard by the inmates, or reach the stables, a drizzling rain began to fall, and as not a vestige of shelter presented itself, it suddenly occurred to me to approach the gate and clamour at the house-bell till I obtained admittance.

"The gate it was easy to make out, but neither bell nor bell-wire could I find.

"Either they had been purposely removed, or the bell rung on our arrival by my companion was suspended to some lofty tree. I might as well have attempted to force my way into a fortress, as into this abominable villa !"——

"You were, in short, a solitary prisoner,

between the garden paling and an impervious wall, exposed to a soaking rain.——What a persecution !"——

" But as if all this, madam, did not suffice, while endeavouring to find the bell, I was startled by a low growl proceeding from the neighbouring bushes, and, on renewing my attempts, two house-dogs, of colossal size, came prowling about my legs, resisting with surly defiance all attempts at conciliation, by hand or voice, in a manner which persons conversant with the demonstrations of canine nature hold far more alarming than a snarl.

" In a fit of desperation, I now snatched at the handle of the gate, when, to my utter amazement, the latch yielded. Without hesitation, I rushed forth. The gate closed behind me with a snap; and finding myself in a lane, and secure at least from the attacks of the gaunt guardians of this trap-hole of a villa, I determined to walk on briskly towards the nearest habitation (which, as far as I could remember, was a small alehouse by the roadside, about a quarter of a mile distant) whence I might despatch a person in quest of a vehicle to take me back; or at all events satisfy my curiosity concerning the originators of the extraordinary hoax of which I was the victim.

"Before I attained the spot, however, I became perplexed by a turning, and taking the way I flattered myself led to the London road, (my hat being slouched over my eyes, and my collar drawn up to my ears as a shelter against the rain) I trudged onwards along a raised causeway, which gradually sank into the road, and became miry almost as a quagmire. Another moment, and I found my feet actually in the water,—a step further, I should have been floating in the cold, dark waters of the Thames.—

"I had attained the river, it seemed, at a spot used as a watering-place for cattle, overhung by the straggling branches of a broken old willow-tree; a most unsafe place for foot-travellers on a starless night. All I had now to do, was to retrace my steps towards the cross-road, on reaching which, I suffered my-self to be again puzzled, again misled.

"To find the well-remembered public-house, however, baffled all my attempts. I passed the gates of several market-gardens, in which there were habitations. But at these, in succession, I rang in vain. The first light I discerned after quitting the hateful villa, was——

"But I humbly entreat your ladyship's pardon," cried Sir Jedediah, interrupting him-self, as he glanced at the timepiece. "I have intruded on your ladyship's time far beyond any reasonable hour of retiring to rest. In the engrossment of my egotism, I forgot that I am addressing an invalid, of whose ailments I am not as yet enabled to form a definite idea. You will, perhaps, permit me to con-sider this a friendly visit, and return to-mor-row afternoon, for a professional investigation of your symptoms? Meanwhile, I rejoice to perceive a sensible diminution of the languor I noticed in your ladyship's appearance on my first entrance. There is a slight effusion of colour on your ladyship's cheek; and your eyes are brightened, at this moment, by a degree of animation, denoting, perhaps, feverish excitement, but which might be mistaken for the looks of a young person in perfect health."

"My spirits have been indeed lightened of a heavy load this evening," said I, ashamed to own how deeply I was interested in his narrative; and how gladly I would have sat up till one in the morning to listen to its conclusion. "It is perhaps owing to the slight stream of air you introduced into the room by opening the window, that I have been thus relieved. I am apt to confine myself to too stagnant an atmosphere."

"On that point, with your ladyship's leave, we will decide to-morrow," said he, rising to take leave, after politely declining the offered fee.

"And on the morrow," cried I, in my turn, almost as much interested as Lady Anne had been herself in the first instance, to hear the conclusion of Sir Jedediah's strange adventure, "what did he suggest?—and above all,

what more did you learn of the extraordinary
people and place with whom he had been thus
singularly brought into collision?"——

"*That* secret constitutes a main portion of
Sir Jedediah's professional Arcanum!" said
Lady Anne, with a provoking smile. "If
you also are suffering from that worst of nervous disorders called *ennui*, you have no right
to pretend to be cured gratis.——Come here
to-morrow at one o'clock, and meet my in-
comparable doctor; you shall then, if you
think proper, learn from his own lips the conclusion of his story. No one but himself can
do justice to the adventure."

This was provoking enough, for I could
only understand her refusal as a hint for dis-
missal; and so excited were my feelings by
all I had heard, and the expressive brilliancy
of her countenance, animated by the interest
of the moment, that I would fain have listened
for hours. But the wax-lights were burning
low; and even Flora got up and stretched
herself, as though to remind me that the hour
of rest for man and beast was at hand.

"One word more, lady fair," said I, as I prepared to take leave. "Did the patient so mysteriously concealed from Sir Jedediah turn out to be——"

"Ask him yourself!" cried Lady Anne, extending her delicate forefinger towards me to be shaken. "Meanwhile, from the eagerness depicted in your countenance, I see that you are as likely to become a convert as myself to the new system; as well as a most capital subject for Sir Jedediah Claversham's system of HOT WATER CURE."

N 5

MAY FAIR AT BRUGES.

A SKETCH.

Let any disciple of Prout, in want of subjects for his pencil, set forth on May-day from
the dingy banks of the Thames ; and fourteen
hours out of sight of unpicturesque London,
he will find a variety of brilliant pictures
awaiting his vivifying brush, in one of the
quaintest old city of Flanders.——The May Fair
of Bruges contains an unexhausted treasury
for the sketch-book.

In the olden time, when Bruges was the
capital of a country the alliance of which appeared so precious to our own, that our kings
gave their daughters in marriage to the Counts
of Flanders, and, in their reverses, were grate-
ful for a refuge at their amphibious court,
London was eager to accept instruction at the
hands of the Flemings in the arts of peace.
Their painters, carvers, and weavers, were

warmly invited over by our less polished
citizens; nor was it till centuries after the
establishment of an Exchange at Bruges,
which then constituted the chief mart of commerce between the Western and Eastern
worlds, that this valuable facilitation of mercantile traffic was emulated in our own and
other countries.

Even at that remote epoch, however—even
before the penniless Edward IV. had paid a
pilot with the pledge of his royal robes to
convey him across the channel to Bruges, (to
the court of Charles the Bold, the husband of
his sister, Margaret of York), even *then*, the
city boasted the very endowment and procession still constituting the attraction of its annual May Fair; and for the space of six
centuries, the quaint old Flemish capital has
thrown itself yearly on its knees, in honour of
a pageant which still excites the amazement
and interest of some thirty thousand of spectators.

The merry month of May is in all countries
the fittest season for a procession.   The skies

are at their bluest, the trees at their greenest,
—the hearts of the populace at their blithest.
Summer is before them with all her gifts of
plenteousness, and Hope by their side; nor
has the sun yet attained a fervour unfavour-
able to out-of-door pastimes. In fixing the
date of the said fair, therefore, and the public
festival therewith connected, the Bruges of
1311 showed itself as wise and weatherwise
as its less prosperous representative, the
Bruges of 1846.

The choice of the epoch, however, had another origin than the wisdom of the legislature.
It was about the same period of the year that
the BLOOD OF CHRIST, in honour of which the
annual festival was instituted, first made its
appearance in Christendom. To revive old
legends in the present day, is a somewhat
thankless office; but when perpetuated by the
reverence of hundreds of thousands of our
contemporaries, and the source of a national
custom sanctified by seven hundred years' observance, they are entitled to our respectful
interest.

In April, 1150, a vial of crystal and gold, containing a few drops of the blood of our Saviour, expressed from the sponge used in his agony by Joseph of Arimathea and Nicodemus, was brought into Europe by Thierry of Alsace, Count of Flanders, one of the most remarkable heroes of the Crusades. In gratitude for his efforts in redemption of the Holy Sepulchre, the King of Jerusalem had bestowed upon him, in presence of the Emperor Conrad and all the chosen chivalry of the West, this precious relic, deposited in the sanctuary of the Holy Chapel, at its endowment, by the Empress Helena; and at the close of the august ceremonial, Thierry, created at the same time Lord of Damascus, consigned the keeping of the vial to Leonius, Abbot of St. Bertin, around whose neck it was suspended by a chain of gold.

Forthwith, this holy man, mounted on a palfrey richly caparisoned, and preceded by two barefooted Carmelites, set forth for Europe, side by side with the Count of Flanders; and, in their progress towards Flanders, multitudes of Christians of all nations and languages, on learning the sacred treasure which the Count and his Flemish knights were bearing to Bruges, rushed forth to meet them by the way. The Holy Blood may be said to have traversed Europe between files of kneeling devotees ; and it is scarcely possible for a relic to be better authenticated, in the eyes of the most fastidious of relic-mongers.

Arrived at Bruges, the precious vial was deposited by Thierry on the altar of the chapel of St. Basil, adjoining his palace ; and an order of priests appointed for its perpetual guardianship.

It was not, however, till the 3rd of May, 1311, that, in consideration of the crowds of pious persons continually thronging to the city for the purpose of saluting so thriceholy a treasure, an annual procession was instituted in its honour.

At first, the Holy Blood, though in a state of congealment, was said to liquify every Friday. For a period of sixty years, we are told, the miracle was in suspension ; but, after

the year 1338, it was found to liquify once in
every year.   In 1617, a magnificent shrine
of gold and precious stones, to the value of
£60,000 sterling, was bestowed upon the
relic, at the cost of thirty-two deacons of
Bruges ; whose coats of arms in rich enamel
may be seen round the base of this costly
shrine, as it is now borne in procession, with
precisely the same forms, and exciting the
same spirit of devotion, as half a dozen centuries ago.

To a protestant eye, the splendours of such
a gaud, and to a protestant mind the value of
such a relic, are of minor account.   But even
a mussulman or brahmin could not fail to be
enchanted by the beautiful aspect of the old
city, with its quaintly-carved Spanish gables
and Gothic traceries ; interspersed for the
occasion, from base to pinnacle, with young
branches of larch and fir, beech and alder,——
their tender verdure contrasting exquisitely
with the old gray stone.   Here and there, a
whole frontage is adorned with bushes of yellow broom from the adjoining woods ; while

the open casements are filled with boughs of
lilac blossoms, or huge pyramids of tulips,
pæonies, and lilies of the valley. It might be
fairly called the festival of flowers; for not a
window of the city (built to contain 200,000
souls, though the population is now reduced
to a fourth of the number) but exhibits a show
of blossoms, in a richness of profusion only
equalled by that of a horticultural show.

The effect would be perhaps enhanced, if
the inhabitants contented themselves with this
single addition to the characteristic *façades*
of their venerable mansions. But every house
insists upon hanging forth its banner or banners ; some displaying a colossal tricolor,
waving from the upper story?——others, flags
of every hue from every window.——In many
streets, rich or fanciful ornaments are slung
across, over the heads of the processionals.
In others, old Flemish tapestries and hangings
of arras cover the entire frontage. Whatever
household ornaments of this description a
Brugeois may possess, are on this occasion put
forth in honour of the grand palladium of his
native city.

Before the door of the burgomaster, for instance (a certain Heer van Huerne van Puyenbeke, whose name has figured in the magistracy of Flanders nearly as long as the sacred relic has graced the chapel of St. Basil), are annually appended a collection of curious webs of ancient tapestry — heirlooms of his house,—interspersed with sconces and tapers; while above the gateway is displayed a noble picture in oils of the early Flemish school, by one of the scholars of Van Eyck, representing a dead Christ; the shutters of the picture being adorned with a series of exquisite family portraits,—burgomasters of the fifteenth century.

The whole city, in short, presents a series of rich and beautiful decorations; the least tasteful or interesting of which is the grand *reposoir* constructed opposite the town-hall, where the relic is first produced for the adoration of the populace from the adjoining chapel of St. Basil.

And what a populace!—An influx of five thousand strangers, poured from the neighbouring villages and distant towns,—from the

west and east by the railroad (a single train
of which, on the recent occasion, deposited
two thousand persons), and from the north
and south by the treckschuyts of the canals.
Multitudes of devotees make their appearance
from Zealand and France; while among the
townspeople of Bruges, the May Fair, char-
tered centuries ago for the accommodation of
pilgrims attending the procession of the Holy
Blood, is hailed as an anniversary of family
reunion and rejoicing.

In addition, therefore, to the usual allowance of Flemish women wearing the hooded
black cloak or *cappe*, or peasants with their
two-horned cap of lace (a modification of the
coëffure of Mary of Burgundy) protruding
from under straw bonnets of singular form,—
of Béguines in the mournful conventual habit
devised for them by their original patroness,
the Countess Joan of Constantinople, by whom
they were privileged to present a coronet of
flowers to the Countesses of Flanders, whenever they entered the city,—of Capuchin
monks with their disciplines tied round their

waists,—of lounging officers of lancers, and
priggish clerks of the tribunals,—thousands
of healthy, hearty, happy-faced peasants from
the environs, appear, leading strings of rosy
children; while the labourers, who have for-
saken the plough in honour of the ceremonial,
and donned their quaintly-cut holiday array,
are seen in troops, bareheaded in the streets,
—some muttering a paternoster, others telling their beads,or reciting a penitential psalm.
For nothing can be more common than for the
village priests to enjoin their penitents, either
as a penance or in token of thanksgiving, to
follow the procession of the Holy Blood at the
May Fair of Bruges.

Of those who are prevented joining it on
the appointed day, it is exacted for days and
weeks afterwards, to follow the course of the
said procession,—pausing and praying where
it halted. For truly, indeed, is it said by
modern travellers, that Belgium is the most
catholic country of Europe.

The ceremonial of the festival of the Holy
Blood commences at midnight the preceding

night; when the relic and shrine (kept all the year round under the guardianship of the canons of St. Basil, submitted to the authority of the Bishop of Bruges) are brought forth and placed upon the altar.—The chapel being illuminated, a solemn mass is said, and anthems are performed throughout the night. At one in the morning, the community of the *Béguines*, headed by their priests, are admitted to kiss the relic; who, on quitting the chapel, proceed in solemn procession, with lighted tapers, round the town, following the course the shrine is to follow next morning; reciting psalms and prayers, and bearing censers, along the *Omgang* between the two ramparts. This ceremony, which purports to purify and sanctify the way for the mighty relic, generally lasts till daybreak : and on the return of the *Béguines*, at sunrise, the great bell of the fine tower of the market-place is tolled, to announce that the vigil is over, and the Festival of the Holy Blood begun.

The celebrated *carillon* of forty-seven bells, which includes four octaves and is said to be

the finest in existence, is now heard chiming
and tolling at intervals in the morning sunshine ; while in the different churches in the
city, eight or nine in number, matins are performed in full choir, the priests officiating in
each in their richest robes of ceremony. In
the church of Nôtre Dame, the gorgeously
gilt tombs of Charles the Bold and his daughter, Mary of Burgundy, are uncovered to the
public gaze ; and at the cathedral, the Bishop
of Bruges, assisted by the Bishops of Ghent
and Liege, solemnizes divine service.

From the different churches, these dignitaries proceed in pompous procession, banners
flying and incense burning, — the priests
chanting as they go — to the chapel of St.
Basil ; where the vial of crystal and gold is
placed in its shrine, the clergy remaining on
their knees during the ceremony; and on is-
suing from the chapel into the great square
fronting the town-hall, the canons, to four of
whom is intrusted the bearing of the resplendent shrine, convey it to the station or
reposoir in the centre, which is surrounded

by a grove of orange-trees, and other fine
evergreens in blossom ; to receive the homage
of the chief authorities of the city, the various
gildes and corporations, assembled there with
their banners ; —— the governor of Western
Flanders, the burgomaster of Bruges, and
detachments of the different regiments in garrison.

Clouds of incense now arise, mingled with
the sonorous chanting of several hundred
priests ; and not only the vast mass of the
populace, but thousands of well-dressed citizens for whose accommodation seats are provided in a semicircle round the station, fall
upon their knees on the stones, the moment
the hallowed relic is uplifted by the venerable
hands of the bishop.

It is from this point and at this moment
the procession begins ; and never perhaps did
it start under more brilliant auspices than on
the 8th of May, 1846. The atmosphere
having been cleared by a slight shower the
preceding evening, the streets were free from
dust, though without losing the spotless and

most Flemish aspect of their neat pavement.
At the first blast of the trumpets, the march
was begun by persons employed by the muni-
cipality to scatter freshly-cut flags and rushes,
mixed with sprigs of broom, along the line,
forming a rich carpet of green and gold ; the
first to trample upon which were the chargers
of a fine brass band of a regiment of lancers,
giving breath to one of Bellini's inspiring
marches, as they rode at a foot's pace across
the square to enter the street leading to the
cathedral.

Next, came the rival band of the cuirassiers,
also riding five abreast ; and, after a pause,
followed the ferocious-looking sapeurs or
pioneers, with their snow-white aprons, and
flowing beards. To these, succeeded the band
and officers of an infantry regiment, marching
to martial music ; and after the infantry, the
band of an Harmonic Association, one of the
best amateur companies in Flanders.

Next came a variety of curious and ancient
banners, displayed by the standard-bearers of
the different *gildes ;* the cross-bowmen, with

their gorgeous St. Sebastian——of which body
our own Charles II. was, during his exile, a
member, —— the long-bowmen, riflemen, and
divers other companies.

A new light now broke in upon the line,
diffused by the *cierges*, or lighted tapers, belonging to the altars of the different churches,
borne on either side by the minor canons; the
clergy and the authorities of the city, preceded
by sergeants-at-arms with their halberds,
marching in full costume and bareheaded in
the centre. To these succeeded an interesting
procession of the charity girls of the different
schools and hospitals of the city, in their neat
dresses of gray serge and snow-white caps
and aprons, escorted by the nuns their preceptresses, and the priests their directors;
each bearing a prayer-book in her hand, and
most of them murmuring their prayers with a
most pious and awe-struck air, as if conscious
of assisting in one of the great mysteries of
their faith.

After the nuns, by whom the children were
headed and followed, came a company of cho-

risters bearing tapers. Then, a long array of young girls, dressed in white, the children of wealthy citizens, in all the pomp of muslin and Flanders lace, wearing white garlands under their long white veils, and exhibiting in their little coquettish glances at the crowded windows of the old Gothic houses, under which the procession was passing, a very different spirit from that of their humbler sisters, under the guidance of their grave preceptresses.

By these aerial-looking creatures, united in line by traces of white ribbons, were borne, two by two, escutcheons inscribed with verses of Scripture in the Flemish language, in white letters, on a pale blue ground, with other devices and emblazonments of pious tendency; many of the escutcheons representing the instruments used in the death and passion of our Sáviour.

The last thirty or forty couple of maidens bore, instead of these grave accessories, baskets of the finest flowers, to scatter over those already trampled by the procession, so as to furnish a fresh surface for the passage of the approaching shrine. The first, however, to profit by it, were a dozen of youthful pages, arrayed in the Flemish garb, preceding the burgomaster, bareheaded, and wearing the decorations of his orders.

A fine strain of chanting now arose on the air; and at this point, the procession, viewed in one of the more ancient streets, (such as Noord Zand Straet, where it pauses before the residence of the burgomaster) assumed its most imposing aspect. The tapestry and banners appended from the carved walls, and the green carpet of verdure under foot, seemed to transform the open causeway into the ancient gallery of some Gothic palace; the fair faces of well-dressed spectators crowding the windows of every story between the gorgeous banners and storied tapestries, as well as the compact throng pressing against the crimson ropes held at intervals by gendarmes to secure free passage for the procession, being alike silent under the influence of deep devotion.

Fumes of incense announced the coming of

the more august portion of the show. The
banners of the different churches, borne by
choristers, seemed to form a canopy above;
while the two white lines of children scatter-
ing flowers appeared to vanish in the distance
on the earth, as the faint echoes of military
music melted into air,—giving place to the
solemn chant of the priests and grave march
of the lay vicars, bearing silver candelabra,
and other consecrated ornaments of the altar;
and an apparently interminable line of priests
belonging to the Episcopal Seminary, bareheaded, their spotless robes of muslin and rich
lace thrown out by the black garments beneath, as those of the choristers by the scarlet, — each reciting the appropriate service
from his open breviary.

More incense, flung from rich censers of
silver,—more tapers,—more banners; among
which, the episcopal standards of Bruges and
Ghent, with their crosiers and mitres! Then,
while the shrill sweet voices of a youthful
choir mingled with the circling fumes of the
incense, appeared the majestic Bishop of

Ghent; his train of cloth of gold, borne by
two dignitaries of the church, in robes of
crimson velvet, gorgeously enriched.

Scarcely had his glittering mitre and the
gaudy array of his attendant priests and deacons ceased to dazzle the eye, when the Bishop
of Bruges, also apparelled in an alb of cloth
of gold, and similarly attended, followed;
when the eye became perplexed between a
desire to follow this gorgeous group, with the
silver lanterns, crosiers, candelabra, and other
massive ornaments of the church, glittering
in the air above their heads like the lances of
an army, winding its way in the distance; or
amid clouds of incense, the coming of the
shrine of shrines.

Already, however, the assembled multitude
was on its knees in reverential silence; and it
would be difficult to do justice to the fervent
faith depicted in the uplifted faces of the
populace, when the splendid canopy of gold
and jewels, under the centre of which, in a
red casket, is deposited the vial of the Holy
Blood, was borne slowly along, on the shoul-

ders of four canons, in the richest array of the Catholic church.

So overpowering is the weight of this gorgeous ornament, that trestle-bearers follow close behind, partly to afford an interval of rest to the dignified bearers; and partly to enable the devout throng to satiate their eyes with a view of what they regard as the most inestimable. of treasures. At that moment, breathless emotion seems to unite the compact multitude into one being; nor is a word uttered so long as the shrine remains in sight.

A detachment of military closes the procession; and immediately upon their horses' heels follow a massive throng of the pilgrims, who, in the course of the year, have made a vow, either in sickness or some great strait or peril, to accompany the procession of the Holy Blood. When compressed into a narrow street, this train of bareheaded, and in some instances barefooted, devotees, seems to "stretch to the crack of doom." In days of yore, pageants or mysteries representing Goliath and the Philistines, Samson and Dalilah, and other scriptural episodes, used to close the array.

When at length all have passed, and the great serpent of the procession has wound its way towards some opposite quarter of the town, so that nothing remains in the street but the trampled flowers and verdure below, the waving banners and rich tapestry above, the green trees and branches clothing the intervals, and the bright garlands and pyramids of flowers at the casements, so recently alive with human faces, and now exhibiting only this pure decoration,——while the musky fragrance of the incense lingering in the air overpowers even the fresher scent of the masses of lilac blossom,—the charm is already so far dispelled, that we ask ourselves with amazement, "*Are* we in sober Flanders, and the nineteenth century, within reach of a railroad and a steam-packet; or have we not suddenly retrograded into the bigotry of the middle ages, and ' eaten of the insane root ' of Italian enthusiasm ?"——

Let wiser men decide upon the good or evil

influence of such usages and institutions, in modifying the character of a people. Certain it is that, though a similar procession would elicit more mirth than admiration from a Parisian throng, and from the higher classes only a polished smile of derision, — in old Flanders it commands nearly the same veneration as under the antique sceptre of the Dukes of Burgundy; and wise and prudent is the government which respects so harmless an expression of popular feeling.

The neighbouring towns and cities are permitted to contribute their choirs and priestly administrants to enhance the augustness of the ceremonial. The garrison and authorities of the city are in enforced attendance; and it is recorded that, for centuries past, the procession has enjoyed untroubled weather, and exemption from the disasters too often attending such multitudinous assemblages.

Meanwhile, for the recreation of the thousands of strangers whose curiosity causes the city to overflow even as the devotion of pilgrims in the olden time, the day is concluded with a variety of entertainments. The bands of the different lyrical societies and *gildes* perform in the afternoon. The cross-bowmen meet in various directions in their shooting-grounds,—the bowmen in theirs;—and for the lower classes, the May Fair, instituted four centuries ago by the Countess Margaret of Flanders, exhibits its booths and shows, its circus of horsemanship, its Lapland family, its dwarfs and giants.

The pious, still penetrated by the sentiments of devotion engendered by the festival of the day, repair for vespers to the cathedral; which is adorned with its utmost pomp, hung with the richest tapestries, and redeemed by the embellishment of innumerable lustres and sconces from the ghastly aspect imparted to Flemish cathedrals by the sepulchral predominance of black and white marble. Or to the church of Nôtre Dame, to pray beside the tombs of their ancient sovereigns, or admire the rich Gothic tribune belonging to the extinct family of Gruthuyse (which figured in our English peerage in 1392, as representative of the earldom of Winchester,) still displaying the Flemish motto so suggestive of noble ambitions, " *meer is in u !*"—" more is in thyself !"   Or to the church of Jerusalem, a fac-simile of the holy sepulchre, created in the thirteenth century by the noble family of Adorri, whose tombs and effigies it enshrines; or to the hospital of St. John, in whose sacristy are preserved the first oil-pictures ever painted, and the last productions of Hemling, unrivalled till the grand discovery of oil-painting.   Be it observed, by the way, that the exquisite pictures of Hemling, whose colours are traditionally recorded in the hospital wherein they were painted to have been composed with gum and white of egg, are as brilliant at the present day as those of his rival, Van Eyck, of whose invention of oil-colours the jealousy of the artist forbade him to avail himself.

The majority, meanwhile, repair to the old gothic chapel of St. Basil,——where the shrine of the Holy Blood has been once more deposited in the guardianship of its clergy,——to press their lips to the sacred vial, or admire the gorgeous workmanship of the *chasse*, executed in 1617, by Jan Crabbe, a burgess of Bruges, a city renowned for its skill in goldsmiths' work.

Adorning the golden canopy which covers the fretted ark containing the relic, is the crown of Mary of Burgundy ; above which is a large pelican of gold and rubies feeding its young. This appears to have been a favourite symbol of divine grace with the Brugeois ; for it not only figures in all their lady chapels, but, on occasion of the forty days' festival which celebrated the union of Margaret of York with Charles the Bold, a pelican of gilt silver was placed in the courtyard of the palace of the Prinzenhof, from the wounded breasts of which issued a fountain of hippocras during the whole time of the entertainment ; —a design not altogether consonant with the refinements of modern taste.

To the artists to whom we have already suggested a visit to the May Fair of Bruges, we venture further to recommend, as studies, the groups of simple-minded peasants of Flanders and Brabant, in their appropriate costumes, gazing with open-eyed wonder upon these marvels; the Blankenbergh fishermen, in their quaint old Spanish dress,——the damsels of Ypres, and Vrouwes of Zealand. Provincial costumes, like other European nationalities, are gradually becoming obsolete ; and the black cloak or *cappe* of Flanders, which is depicted in bas-reliefs of the tenth century nearly of the same form as worn at the present day, would doubtless also be laid aside, but for the exigencies of the climate.

A Flemish crowd clustered round one of the booths or merry-go-rounds of the May Fair of Bruges, with the ancient Venetian-looking Halle as the background of the picture, —— or crossing one of the innumerable bridges that give their Flemish name of *Brug* to the city, overlooked by some old gabled mansion of Spanish architecture, unchanged since the days of Charles V.,——nay, many of still more ancient origin, and contemporary

with the Arteveldes themselves,——is a treasure
for the study of the colourist, as well as a solace for the antiquarian.

Hapless, however, the city which is able to
preserve such institutions as the procession of
the Holy Blood, or exhibit dwellings and costume unchanged by the lapse of half a dozen
centuries !——The want of energy, the want of
enlightenment, the want of progress demon-
strated by such immutability, accounts for its
abandonment by the higher classes, who furnish the sustenance of the lower.

Bruges, as it has been already stated, is
nearly deserted !   Since the origin of the procession we have described, the number of its
inhabitants has dwindled by three-fourths.
Its looms of tapestry have ceased to exist;
even its lace-trade is becoming extinct.   The
city, whose master-weavers were eagerly de-
coyed by Edward III., and which used to furnish the Gobelins with their most expert
artists, has not one left for its own purposes;
——and the city which executed the celebrated chimney-piece of the Palais de Justice,

still visited as a *chef d'œuvre* by the artists of
Europe, boasts neither carver nor sculptor !——
Its learned men seek refuge in more en-
lightened countries. The royal library of
Paris possesses itself of the valuable services
of a Van Praêt ; and, like another Niobe,
Bruges stands disconsolate, bereft of her chil-
dren.

Hence, still increasing declension ;——hence,
foundations ploughed by ignorance and super-
stition in the furrowed cheeks of time, for
trivial observances and all the mummeries of
priestcraft. If the arts still find their account
in these antiquated monuments and exploded
ostentations, like the rich vegetation springing
from the disjointed stones of some ancient
structure, it is regarded by the sober eye of
reason as affording only a melancholy indica-
tion of decay.

But, before the old gables of the house of
Gruthuyse and other relics of the fourteenth
and fifteenth centuries crumble into the slug-
gish canals at their feet, may our galleries
obtain reminiscences of the old city, embel-

lished by all the sunshine, verdure, and diver-
sification attending the procession of the Saint
Sang, and the joyous pageantry of its May
Fair!——

HUSH!

Wheatham is a pleasant village in the county of Herts, — a village of smock-frocks, straw-plaiting, and pleasant faces ; having on its outskirts the usual Hertfordshire allowance of Parklets, Lodges, and " Genteel residences," with taking titles, so apt to figure in the windows of house-agents, annexed to seductive sketches in water-colours of rural *otium cum dignitate*, every way worthy to figure in the Suffolk Street Gallery.

Of these country-seats,—nearly as shiftful of their proprietors as seats in parliament,— the grandest was decidedly Wheatham Priory ; about as much of a priory, by the way, as the Freemasons' Tavern ; having been built, " from turret to foundation-stone," or rather from foundation-stone to turret, within the last ten years.

Instead of pretending to the dim religious
light accordant with the sacred title it arrogated
to itself, it combined all orders of architecture
with all varieties of style ;——being constructed
in poppy-coloured brick, after the fashion of
Fortnum's Temple of sugar and spice in Pic-
cadilly, and Hampton Court Palace; one of
those hybrid monstrosities that annually dis-
figure the Architectural Room at the Royal
Academy, among commemorations of other
lions of the year,——Dwarknauth Tagore, the
chimpanzee, or the giraffes.——

New as it was, however, Wheatham Priory
was the property of a master still newer than
itself. The construction of this barbarous
edifice had, as usual, ruined the retired cit for
whom it had been originally designed ; and,
instead of residing under the battlemented
roof of his nondescript priory, the old pin-
maker had been so fortunate as to escape the
Queen's Bench by retreating into a more modest home, in Wheatham churchyard. The
scarlet abomination had, in consequence, come
to the hammer ; which, though unable to do

the kindness to the neighbourhood of knocking
it down altogether, had knocked it down, for
the time being, to the possession of that distinguished member of the Common Council,
Mr. Gamaliel Cribbs, of Gracechurch Street.

The quiet neighbourhood of Wheatham
heaved a deep sigh on hearing that, in addition to the eyesore of what the villagers familiarly called " the red house," it was about to
be afflicted with the company of a man whom
the newspapers, and his own litigious, frac-
tious, and interfering officiousness, rendered
so notorious in the annals of city legislation.

For it was a sociable and tranquil district ;
free from the envyings and heart-burnings too
often arising in English country neighbour-
hoods from pretension to the favour of some
adjacent ducal castle, or lordly hall. There
was not so much as the coronet of a viscount
or viscountess within ten miles round, to furnish a golden apple of discord ; and the arrival of the pompous Mr. Gamaliel Cribbs, in
his lake-coloured family-coach, was accordingly hailed with sore misgivings and regret.

Nevertheless, all the duties of country-neighbourship were discharged in a truly Christian spirit towards the new-comers. Cards and visits,—visits and cards,—and, in process of time, dinner-parties and tea-parties, afforded occasion to Mr. and Mrs. Cribbs to exhibit their hospitalities in return; and, as had been anticipated, the exhibition was effected in a style intended to strike humiliation into the hearts of those whom the dignities of the castellated priory had heretofore failed to intimidate. Turtle and venison smoked upon the board of the Common-councilman; and, lest the new little succession houses of the new little country-seat should be put to the blush by the forcing-houses of Ashridge or Brocket, such pines and peaches arrived, per coach, from Covent Garden, as might have been supposed to arrive from the garden of the Hesperides.

By all this unneighbourly ostentation, poor little Wheatham felt considerably oppressed. It had no longer courage to invite the great man, whose plate out-glittered the sunshine,

to its homely tea-parties and family-dinners.
Its sociable spirit sank rebuked.   The bows
and curtsies exchanged at church with Mr.
and Mrs. Gamaliel Cribbs, instead of becoming
more cordial on a closer acquaintance, grew
colder, or more reserved.   One or two elderly
spinsters, of small means, wondered at their
own audacity in having attempted so august
an acquaintance, and withdrew from the field ;
and it was only the good vicar, Doctor Monson, and his warm-hearted wife, who, regarding the Cribbses as absurd people, with whom,
as parishioners, it was their duty to be indul-
gent, remained on the same terms as ever with
Wheatham Priory.   Associating familiarly
with the old-established families of the county,
the Monsons contented themselves with re-
gretting the bad taste of their rich neighbours ; hoping that the crumbs which fell
from their table might prove at least a bless-
ing to the poor.
    In this, however, they were mistaken. Ga-
maliel, like most ostentatious people, was a
bitter economist.   He did not suffer crumbs

to *exist* in his establishment.   The loaves and
fishes were weighed in the balance ; and, if
found wanting by the fraction of a penny-
weight, the quarter-sessions would have heard
of it !

Scarcely was the city man established in
his Poppy-hall, when prodigious placards were
exhibited at intervals on the outskirts of his
estate of seven-and-thirty acres, warning off
trespassers, and threatening man and beast
with the utmost rigour of the law.   But, to
the surprise,——almost to the disappointment,
——of the new landed proprietor, neither beast
nor man defied his enactments !

Either the morals of the parish were kept
in too good repair by the worthy vicar, or the
terrors attached to the name of the Common-
councilman had penetrated as far as the rural
district of Wheatham ; for not so much as a
withered stick disappeared from his hedges.
The snowy mushroom sprang untouched in his
meadows, within half a foot of a public path-
way ; and even the chaffinches seemed to
think twice of the matter before they took

a peck at the hips, haws, or sloes of Wheatham Priory.

Such, in short, was the pacific character of the parish, that for three long years did Gamaliel divide his time between Gracechurch Street and his "genteel residence," without having been able to prosecute a single offender, or so much as to impound a stray donkey! His legal fangs might as well have been extracted, or his claws pared to the quick, for any use they proved to him in the county of Herts. No one chose to rob him; no one chose to quarrel with him. The mild vicar allowed him to say his say unanswered, when he talked nonsense; and, as oil is said to be the most efficient antidote against the bite of a reptile, the quiet acquiescence of the neighbourhood rendered innocuous the arbitrary temper of the city *energumen*.

All this was becoming prodigiously provoking to Cribbs the Cantankerous. He longed for a little opposition, a little bickering, to keep up his spirits. On the eve of retiring from active life, he could not look

forward without uneasiness to spending the
remainder of his days in a place where, as no
one interfered with him, he was unprivileged
to interfere with any.   The spirit of conten-
tiousness waxed hot within him.   He would
have given much to detect some idle lad of
the neighbourhood fishing for minnows in his
duckpond, or seeking birds'-nests in his hedges,
in order to justify a lawyer's letter.   But both
high and low knew better; the Master Mer-
tons, because they had duckponds and hedges
of their own; the Master Sandfords, because
an excellent village-school attested the wise
providence of the vicar.——

He was beginning to fear that he had chosen
ill for his future happiness; that, further from
town, a more lawless population might have
called into action his legislative powers, enabling him to find fault and occupation; when,
lo! a happy source of discord presented itself,
under a form most harmonious.

The organ of Wheatham church, which was
now a century old, and had been half a century out of order, was arriving at so asthmatic

a pitch of disablement, that at times it required all the good feeling prevalent in so well-regulated a parish to preserve decorous gravity in the congregation during the psalmodial portions of divine service !

Truth to tell, the organist had grown old with the organ ; the musician and his instrument being so well assimilated in their infirmities, that it was difficult to separate old Blowpipe from the wheezing organ, in strictures upon its demerits : and, as the old man had spent the whole of his respectable days in the parish, had tuned its pianos for the space of threescore years, and instructed the damsels of four succeeding generations in the art of fingering, he had so many kindly patronesses and champions among the fair Wheathamites, that the flats which ought to have been naturals, and the naturals which ought to have been sharps, passed generously unheard.

Shortly, however, after the transfer of the priory to the hands of the arbitrary cit, the poor old man underwent a stroke of palsy ;

and it was only because ably represented in
the organ-loft by young Alfred Blowpipe, one
of his grandsons, that he escaped being removed from his functions, in favour of a more
efficient performer.

But the modernized skill of the young artist
served only to render still more disagreeably
apparent the defects of the organ ; half of
which had been previously attributed to the
tremulous hand of the superannuated organist.
Poor Alfred strove hard to make the best of
it. For the height of his ambition was to
succeed the head of the family in his office ;
the stipend of which, added to his earnings,
and the consequence of which tending to increase them, would, he flattered himself, enable him to fulfil the dearest wish of his heart,
and claim the hand of pretty Mary Gray, only
daughter of the village schoolmistress.

His prospects as regarded this prefer-
ment were good ; for the vicar, whose married
daughters had been drilled through their Stei-
belt by old Blowpipe, favoured his preten-
sions ; and on summer evenings, it was a

pleasant recreation to poor Alfred to saunter with Mary and her mother through the beautiful green lanes and outskirts of the luxuriant cornfields of Wheatham, indulging in delightful dreams of future domesticity.

Of late, these visions had received a charming acceleration from a hint let fall by Dr. Monson, that, if the harvest should prove so good as to afford the certainty of a prosperous winter to secure the parish from extraordinary appeals to its beneficence, he would propose a subscription for a new organ; in consequence of which contingent condition, Mary Gray became as careful an observer of the vicissitudes of the weather and state of the crops, as though she had possessed landed property rivalling the mighty estates of Gamaliel Cribbs, Esq. Whenever the sun shone, Mary smiled; whenever the rain fell over-abundantly, Mary wept,—till the poor girl's face became a perfect weather-glass!

Luckily, however, the skies were propitious! —It rained only when rain was wanting, and shone only when sunshine was in request; and

before the close of July, so plentifully were
the garners of Wheatham filled with their
golden store, that it was as much as Alfred
Blowpipe could do, *not* to convert his volun-
taries at matins and even-song into jigs and
strathspeys.   The heart of the young organist
was glad within him.

The vicar was as good as his word, and his
word was excellent.   Early in the month of
August, an extraordinary meeting of the vestry was called; and Mumps, the church-
warden, having contrived to whisper its pur-
port in various directions, the parish was
tolerably in the secret of the proposition about
to be laid before its thrones and dominions.
Unfortunately enough, as it happened;—for
the great Gamaliel Cribbs was fated to receive the first hint of it from the officious and
facetious stationer of Wheatham who had the
honour of supplying the Priory with wafers
and packthread (in order, as the great man
frequently observed, to afford a little patron-
age to " the people on his estate "); whereas,
had Dr. Monson made an express visit of

communication on the subject to his wealthy parishioner, a new organ would have formed an especial and exclusive gift from the Priory; the benefaction being duly commemorated in letters of gold upon the front of the instrument.

But the Common-councilman had no notion of being less in Dr. Monson's confidence than Wirewove, the stationer. The Common-councilman felt that Wheatham Priory was entitled to the deference of Wheatham vicarage; and before he reached the scarlet lodge of his little domain on the sultry afternoon when the irritating communication was first conveyed, he had made up his mind to get up an opposition to Dr. Monson's project, or, as *he* phrased it, " to let the parson see he wasn't the man to be bamboozled."

When the vestry met, accordingly, and, in his usual simple and friendly tone, the vicar communicated his intention to appeal to the liberality of the parish for the renewal of the organ and permanent appointment of Alfred Blowpipe in place of his infirm grandfather,

P 2

to whom he was to make an adequate allowance out of his stipend, Gamaliel up and
spoke,—spoke loud and long,—and, unhap-
pily, in the tone of plausibility and authority
which a long habit of factious oratory enabled
him readily to assume.

"The wants of the people," "the necessities of the poor," "the disasters of the times,"
"the serious duty of those intrusted with the
distribution of the parochial funds," were
successively enlarged upon. "For *his* part,"
he said, "he fully agreed with his esteemed
friend, Dr. Monson, that no point should be
left unconsidered by thinking minds, which
tended to enhance the attraction of divine
worship to those lukewarm Christians less inclined than could be wished to devotional
practices. God forbid," he observed, "that
any portion, however trivial, of the church
service should be neglected in the parish to
which he belonged. But he would only ask
the worthy friends and colleagues he had the
pleasure of addressing, whether it was becoming, in times like the present, to take the

children's bread, and give it unto the dogs?
Whether there was any pretext or excuse for
putting the parish to an enormous expense for
the purchase of a musical instrument, when
one of less cost, but abundantly sufficient for
their purpose, might be had.

"Above all," he asked, "how were they
to settle it with their consciences if they sad-
dled a parish far from easy in its circumstances
with the gnawing worm of a permanent organist, at the high salary of forty or fifty
pounds per annum; at a period when, thanks
to the march of intellect and progress of civili-
zation, the finest music extant was the result
of machinery! What was the Apollonicon,
he should like to know?——He would under-
take to say that cylinder organs satisfied the
parochial ambition of nine out of every ten
parishes of the calibre of Wheatham!——Cylinder organs neither ate, nor drank, nor slept.
——Cylinder organs were not subject to para-
lytic strokes.——The first cost was the sole cost.
——Any rational being (that worthy man, for
instance, Jones, the sexton, who maintained a

large family without the aid of parochial relief) would be overjoyed to turn the organ of
Wheatham for a sum of sixpence per hour,——
say five pounds per annum; which would
leave a bonus of five and forty pounds annually in favour of the parish, to say nothing of
the hundred, or hundred and twenty pounds,
economized in the prime cost of the instrument.   This was a matter for their serious,
——their *very* serious consideration.   It was
not a subject to be dealt with so lightly as
some people seemed to imagine: All admi-
nistrative duties, from the highest to the
lowest, from the greatest to the least, were
delegations from Providence to the consciences
of responsible Christians.

   " What would be their emotions, he wished
to inquire, when the howling tempests of a
severe winter shook their habitations about
their ears, conveying the terrible certainty
that hundreds of their fellow-parishioners were
shivering with cold,——cold aggravated by mi-
sery and famine,——and they reflected that the
money, which might have secured warmth and

comfort to these afflicted creatures, had been squandered on the futile purpose of tickling the ears of certain persons, whose piety was of so equivocal a nature that they could not worship their Maker without the stimulus of an accessory which, to the truly pious, was as the sounding brass and tinkling cymbal! *The deaths of these suffering Christians,—if death should ensue,— would lie at their door !*—He would say no more.   He confessed himself to be overcome by the consciousness of his moral and parochial responsibilities."

  · He said no more, but he had said more than enough.   His big words and solemn utterance bewildered the wits of the half dozen farmers accustomed to the simple delivery of the vicar. Cylinders carried the day. Machinery *versus* labour had the verdict in its favour.   The parish discovered that it could not possibly afford an outlay of more than fifty pounds for so trivial an acquisition ; and Gamaliel Cribbs, Esq., was accordingly deputed to treat with Messrs. Grindwell and Co.

  That evening, poor Alfred had not courage

to propose to Mary and her mother their
usual stroll along the green lanes !——All three
sat silent and sorrowful in the school-house,
pretending to contemplate a beautiful nosegay
of exotics which the young man had brought
from the nurseryman's, (to whose progeny he
officiated as musical preceptor) to console his
plighted wife for the loss of their accustomed
rural pleasures.

And lo ! before the end of the week, their
dreary prospects and bitter disappointments
were confirmed by news that the squire of the
Priory had added to the sum of money de-
creed for the purchase of an organ a further
sum of fifty pounds,——in order to secure the
parish against the salary of an organ-grinder,
by the acquisition of a self-playing organ !——

A self-playing organ !——Such an invention
had never before been heard of in that simple
district ; and the vestry had some difficulty in
bringing itself to understand how the united
efforts of the Blowpipes, old and young, could
ever be sufficiently superseded by means of
wheels and levers.   All Wheatham was in a

state of excitement; more especially when
there arrived, in process of time, from town,
a well appointed van, containing a highly-
varnished mahogany organ, no more resem-
bling the old one, than a showy captain of
lancers resembles my Uncle Toby;——escorted
by a young gentleman of dandified aspect,
who was to superintend the setting up of the
new instrument, officiate for the first Sunday
or two as its master of the ceremonies, and,
in the interim, instruct Jones, the gravedigger,
in the art and mystery of the stops, and adap-
tation of tunes.

So tremendous a state of excitement had
never before convulsed the peaceful bosom of
Wheatham ! When Sunday came, it seemed
no longer the holy Sabbath in the observance
of which the Wheathamites had been trained
by the mild schooling of the vicar. It was
a day to rush to church and listen, *not* to the
exhortations of the pulpit, but the piping of
the organ-loft !——

On that memorable Sunday, Alfred Blowpipe took his seat, for the first time, in the

midst of the congregation, as a private individual, with all the concealed heartburnings
of an ex-minister appearing at court for the
first time in presence of his successor in office.
And lucky was it for the Christian responsibilities of the displaced organist that his jea-
lousies and resentments were expended only
on a thing of wood and leather ; for, had the
gentleman in such well-varnished boots, and
so excessively frilled a shirt as he who set the
machine in motion, been a permanent inflic-
tion on the parish, Alfred would certainly
have been moved to perform his weekly devotions in the adjoining parish, to avoid the
grievance of beholding his rival ascend offi-
cially into the organ-loft.   His sole consolation consisted in the fact that his poor old
grandfather's infirmities of mind and body secured *him* from the knowledge that his humble kingdom was taken from him.

Meanwhile, the service, though read with
his accustomed severe gravity by Dr. Monson,
failed to produce its usual influence on the
congregation, which was restless and inqui-

sitive as the audience of a London theatre on
the night of a new play.   It was evidently a
relief to all present when the moment arrived
for the exhibition of the miraculous powers of
the showy novelty that figured in the gallery.
Before the psalm-books of the public could be
opened, everybody was on foot; and when
the mellifluous tones of the really excellent
organ were heard in the church, so long dis-
graced by the discordant wheezings of the old
one, even Alfred was astonished!   He could
not have believed that so excellent a mechanical substitute could be provided for the
taste and skill, on the exercise of which depended his daily bread; and while the hearts
of all other persons present were elevated by
the sound, his own became depressed to despair.——The organist's occupation was gone!

Throughout the ensuing week, Wheatham
was in ecstasies of gratitude towards the judi-
cious munificence of the Priory; and Gamaliel Cribbs progressed from house to house,
(that is, to every house saving the vicarage)
reaping a harvest of thanks and praise.   Had

the little town been a great borough, and its
representation vacant, Gamaliel would un-
questionably have been its man.   Everybody
was avowedly longing for Sunday.   Everybody, while applauding the far-sighted wisdom which had saved a sum of sixty pounds
per annum to the parish, expressed a degree
of musical enthusiasm in favour of the self-
playing organ, which they would never have
expressed in favour of the finest instrument
turned out by Flight and Robson, and played
by human hands.——

Such is the envious jealousy of our nature !
——There was no reserve to their enthusiasm
in honour of a mere piece of mechanism !——
For even the London master of the ceremonies had returned to the place from whence
he came ; the organ being fixed and paid for ;
——the organ, with its twenty-four psalms and
anthems, to which the parish of Wheatham
was to listen in content and quietness for the
remainder of its days.——

Tears were in the eyes of Mary Gray as she
took her place in her pew, and knew that the

young voices of her mother's scholars were to
be no longer attuned by the masterly aid of
her future husband. She was careful never
once to glance towards the organ in the course
of the service. She could not have borne to
behold Jones, the sexton, attired in his Sunday clothes, in the place of her beloved
Alfred !

The first psalm was sung ;—and no one
present could believe that the youthful voices
by which the new organ was accompanied
were the same which had appeared to utter
" harsh discords and unpleasing sharps," when
united with the mumbling, broken-down bel-
lows of preceding Sundays ; nor, to their
shame be it spoken, could Alfred or Mary
sufficiently restrict their attention to the
Communion Service that ensued, to avoid perceiving that the Cribbs family had drawn
aside the crimson curtains of their pew, to
expose themselves to the approving and grate-
ful glances of the congregation ;—nay, that,
during the performance of the anthem, Gamaliel had uplifted himself upon his hassock,

the better to enjoy the sense of his growing popularity. Poor Mary prayed heartily to be delivered from temptation,—the temptation of loving her neighbour less than herself, or, rather, less than Alfred, whom she loved *as* herself.——

The second psalm commenced, — "four verses *of* the morning hymn" being duly announced by the clerk, and duly taken up by the children, much to the approbation of all present. As usual, in the course of the third verse, Dr. Monson, attired in his gown, ascended the pulpit, where, in the solemn duties of the moment, he lost all thought of factious parishioners or harmonious organs;——and at the concluding line of the last verse opened his sermon, and awaited only the reclosing of the psalm-books of his flock, to commence his solemn adjuration.

But though the psalm-books closed as he expected, the strain of the organ did *not !*—— Another verse, to which, of course, there was no vocal accompaniment, succeeded, after the congregation had reseated itself.

"A little over-zeal on the part of poor Jones!"—thought the vicar. "Before next Sunday, I will warn him to cease with the singing."

And once more, at the conclusion of the verse, he prepared himself to resume his duty. But, alas! the organ chose to resume also,— once, twice, and again; till, after it had performed no less than four gratuitous verses, the vicar beckoned to his clerk, desiring him to inform Jones that he had given them more than enough.

A few minutes afterwards, a message to Dr. Monson from his agonized delegate apprized the poor vicar that the organ had got the best of it; that, owing to the mismanagement of the inexperienced sexton, the stops were embarrassed; and that there was no putting an end to the performance till the unruly instrument had gone through its twelve repetitions of the hymn!

Inexpressibly vexed, (for the congregation was a more numerous one, and collected from greater distances, than it had ever been his

fortune to behold within those walls) Dr.
Monson sat down and resigned himself.

But, though the gravity of his functions
prevented *his* entering into the ludicrous side
of the question, all present were not equally
forbearing.   At every renewal of the hymn,
slight titterings were heard, and the vicar
was beginning to count with anxious feelings
the repetitions of the performance ; when lo !
just as, at the close of the twelfth verse, he
began to breathe more freely and find himself
once more at ease in his own pulpit, where
his mind had never known disturbance before,
the concluding semibreve of the rebellious
organ had scarcely exhausted its swelling
breath, when a *new* strain commenced,—the
EVENING HYMN !——

Twelve verses of the evening hymn !——This
time, the giggling of the juvenile portions of
the population of Wheatham proved past all
power of suppression; and though two naughty
boys, whose merriment had burst into a guffaw,
were thrust out of the porch by the beadle,
with threatenings of a whipping on the mor-

row, the tittering of the charity school was as though a thousand swallows' nests were rearing their young in the roof.——

The case was now imminent. Dr. Monson, inexpressibly anxious lest the awkwardness of such a catastrophe should desecrate the sacred spot he had so long preserved in odour of sanctity, despatched a message to Alfred Blowpipe, requesting him to lend his immediate aid in remedying the difficulty. But, alas ! the report of the ex-organist was fully as discouraging as that of the clerk. The handle of the stop-bolt had been wrested off by the untutored hand of Jones, the sexton ; and there was no possibility of silencing the organ, till it had gone through its *twelve times twenty-four tunes !*——a performance which, on a moderate calculation, would last till dark !

One only remedy suggested itself. A slip of paper, forwarded by the dismayed Gamaliel Cribbs, reminded the vicar that, the four sturdy carpenters being present by whom the organ had been placed in the loft, nothing would be easier than for them to remove it,

and carry it forth into the churchyard, *till*
the conclusion of divine service !

After a moment's deliberation, the vicar, in
the interests of his sermon, thought fit *to*
comply ; and by a group of stalwart Wheathamites, vying in proportions with Irish
chairmen, was the hapless gift of the discom-
fited Gamaliel removed from its high estate,
and carried out of church, like a crying child ;
——more than one grave old farmer finding it
necessary to conceal his laughter behind his
straw hat during the operation, and more than
one youngster exploding into ungovernable
merriment.

Mary Gray alone, with downcast eyes, and
the corners of her mouth quivering between
mirth and tears of joy, sat thanking Providence for the unlooked-for mischance.

No sooner was the gravity of the congregation decently restored, than the distressed
vicar gave out his text.   But even now, all
was not as it should be.   The churchyard
was a small one ; and from beneath the
spreading yew at its extremest verge, under

which the loquacious organ had been placed for shelter, it was heard at intervals babbling on, like Demosthenes declaiming in solitary eloquence on the seashore.

After every full stop of the sermon, as the voice of the vicar paused, that of.the persevering organ became audible at a distance. And again the titterings were renewed, and again the preacher became perplexed, till he found it best to come to an abrupt conclusion, and dismiss his flock, as he had already dismissed the refractory instrument.

In short, St. .Cecilia prospered her own ! For it need hardly be added that, after a disaster which called forth the witticisms of the dullest of county chronicles, and finally reached the wags of the London journals, Wheatham and the Wheathamites were moved to get up a memorial in favour of a finger-organ and resident organist.

Exchange, which was no robbery, enabled them to accomplish their purpose; and whenever any of my readers feel inclined for a quiet Sunday's devotions, they will find Dr. Mon-

son still in the pulpit,——Alfred Blowpipe in
the organ-loft,——and *Mrs. Alfred* presiding
over the head of the village-school, in place of
her infirm mother.

Gamaliel Cribbs has taken a house at Mar-
gate, where he usually passes his summers.
Since " the royal feast for Persia, won by
Philip's warlike son," never was the benig-
nant protection of St. Cecilia more *auspi-*
ciously manifested, than in favour of the
young organist of Wheatham !——

END OF VOL. II.

F. Shoberl, Jun., Printer to H.R.H. Prince Albert, Rupert Street.